BRITAIN'S
MILITARY AIRCRAFT
IN COLOUR
1960 – 1970
Volume 1

BRITAIN'S MILITARY AIRCRAFT IN COLOUR

1960 – 1970

Volume 1

MARTIN DERRY

First published in Great Britain in 2010 by
Crécy Publishing

ISBN 9 780955 426827

Printed in China

Crécy Publishing Limited
1a Ringway Trading Estate
Shadowmoss Road
Manchester M22 4LH

www.crecy.co.uk

Front cover: *Hunter FGA.9 'D' of No.1 Squadron from West Raynham, Norfolk on 16 July 1965.* Author's collection.

Back cover:

Top: *Vampire T.11 XH322, from the Central Flying School, seen at Bruntingthorpe, Leicestershire, on 28 May 1960. Delivered in March 1956, XH322 served briefly with No.500 Squadron - presumably until the Royal Auxiliary Air Force disbanded in March 1957. Thereafter it served with the CFS and was struck off charge on 27 August 1962 and scrapped.* Newark Air Museum

Centre left: *An unidentified Hunter belonging to No.54 Squadron. Further details appear in the caption on page 39.*

Artwork: *Profile artwork for Canberra B.2 WH703. Full four-view artwork for this aircraft can be found on page 92, with supporting photographs and captions on page 83.*

Bottom left: *Valetta T.3 WJ481. An earlier photograph and a summary of this aircraft's history appears on page 18. Comparison of the two images show that WJ481had received, externally at least, a thorough overhaul by the time that this photograph was taken. Unfortunately, details of the date and location are not known.* Newark Air Museum

Bottom right: *Canberra T.17 WJ986. Further details of which appear in the caption on page 94.*

CONTENTS

Abbreviations   6

Introduction   7

1 Vickers Valetta   10

2 Hawker Hunter   24

3 De Havilland Vampire T.11   64

4 English Electric Canberra (Part 1)   76

ABBREVIATIONS AND BIBLIOGRAPHY

A&AEE	Aircraft & Armament Experimental Establishment
AFDS	Air Fighting Development Squadron
AES	Air Electronics School
AFS	Advanced Flying School
ANS	Air Navigation School
APC	Armament Practice Camp
APS	Armament Practice Station
AWRE	Air Weapons Research Establishment
BAC	British Aircraft Corporation
BCCS	Bomber Command Communications Squadron
BCDU	Bomber Command Development Unit
BDRF	Battle Damage Repair Flight
CAACU	Civilian Anti-Aircraft Co-operation Unit
CATCS	Central Air Traffic Control School
CGS	Central Gunnery School
CF	Communication Flight; often prefixed with location e.g. Aden CF
CFE	Central Fighter Establishment
CFS	Central Flying School
CNCS	Central Navigation and Control School
CS	Communication Squadron; often prefixed with location e.g. Colerne CS
CSDE	Central Servicing Development Establishment
CSE	Central Signals Establishment
DFCS	Day Fighter Combat Squadron
DFLS	Day Fighter Leaders School
ECM	Electronic Counter Measures
ETPS	Empire Test Pilots School
FCS	Fighter Combat School (a component of the CFE)
FCIRS	Fighter Command Instrument Rating Squadron
FRADU	Fleet Requirements & Air Direction Unit
FRU	Fleet Requirements Unit
FTS	Flying Training School
FWS	Fighter Weapons School
MoA	Ministry of Aviation
MoD(PE)	Ministry of Defence (Procurement Executive)
MoS	Ministry of Supply
MU	Maintenance Unit
OCU	Operational Conversion Unit
RAE	Royal Aircraft Establishment (Royal Aerospace Establishment from 1st April 1988)
RAFC	Royal Air Force College
RAFCAW	Royal Air Force College of Air Warfare
RAFFC	Royal Air Force Flying College
RRE	Radar Research Establishment
SOC	Struck Off Charge
SoTT	School of Technical Training
TACAN	TACtical Air Navigation
TAF	Tactical Air Force e.g. 2TAF - 2nd Tactical Air Force
THUM Flt	Temperature and HUMidity Flight
TRE	Telecommunications Research Establishment
TT	Target Tug
TWU	Tactical Weapons Unit

Aircraft In British Military Service, since 1946. *Airlife Publishing Ltd*

Aircraft of the RAF. *Putnam & Company Ltd*

Bomber Squadrons of the RAF. *MacDonald and Janes Ltd*

Britain's Military Training Aircraft, The History of. *Haynes Publishing Group*

British Military Aircraft Serials 1878-1987. *Midland Counties Publications*

British Military Aviation, The 1960s In Colour No.1. *Dalrymple & Verdun Publishing*

Broken Wings. Post-War RAF Accidents. *Air-Britain (Historians) Ltd*

Category Five. A Catalogue of RAF Aircraft Losses 1954-2009. *Nimbus Publishing*

Coastal, Support and Special Squadrons of the RAF. *Jane's Publishing Co. Ltd*

Cold War Shield, RAF Fighter Squadrons 1950-1960. *Published by Roger Lindsay*

Cold War Years, Flight Testing at Boscombe Down 1945-1975, The. *Hikoki Publications*

Combat Codes...since 1938. *Airlife Publishing Ltd*

De Havilland Aircraft since 1909. *Putnam & Company Ltd*

De Havilland Vampire, Venom and Sea Vixen. *Ian Allan Ltd*

De Havilland Vampire. *Hall Park Books Ltd*

English Electric Canberra. *Midland Counties Publications*

English Electric Canberra, Part 1. *Aviation Workshop Publications Ltd*

Fighter Squadrons of the RAF. *MacDonald and Janes Ltd*

Final Landings. A Summary of RAF Aircraft and Combat Losses 1946-1949. *Nimbus Publishing*

Fleet Air Arm Fixed-Wing Aircraft since 1946. *Air-Britain (Historians) Ltd*

Fly Navy, Aircraft of the Fleet Air Arm since 1945. *Airlife Publishing Ltd*

Flying Training And Support Units. *Air-Britain (Historians) Ltd*

Flying Units of the RAF. *Airlife Publishing Ltd*

Gloster Javelin, the RAF's First Delta Wing Fighter. *Dalrymple & Verdun Publishing*

Hastings, Handley Page's Post-War Transport Aircraft. *Dalrymple & Verdun Publishing*

Hawker Aircraft since 1920. *Putnam & Company Ltd*

Hawker Hunter. Biography of a thoroughbred. *Patrick Stephens Ltd*

Hunter Squadrons of the RAF and Fleet Air Arm. *Linewrights Ltd*

Last Take-Off. A Record of RAF Aircraft Losses 1950-1953. *Nimbus Publishing*

Names With Wings. *Airlife Publishing Ltd*

Royal Air Force Aircraft, serial monographs (various). *Air-Britain (Historians) Ltd*

Royal Air Force Germany since 1945. *Midland Publishing*

Squadrons of the Fleet Air Arm, The. *Air-Britain (Historians) Ltd*

Squadrons of the Royal Air Force & Commonwealth, The. *Air-Britain (Historians) Ltd*

Under B Conditions. *Merseyside Aviation Society Publications*

Vickers Aircraft since 1908. *Putnam & Company Ltd*

Wrecks & Relics, 21st Edition. *Crecy Publishing*

Wrecks & Relics - The Album. *Midland Publishing*

INTRODUCTION

This book, together with subsequent volumes, is intended to offer a nostalgic selection of colour images with each featuring four types of aircraft in British military, or Ministry service and concentrates predominantly on the period 1960 to 1970 when most of the photographs were taken. However, exceptions occur on either side of the given dates, particularly with the Hawker Hunter and English Electric Canberra, both of which enjoyed exceptionally long periods of service. Full advantage has been taken of a relatively scarce photographic opportunity from a period when a roll of colour film (20 exposures) cost approximately £5, excluding the cost of development; a significant sum in the early 1960s. Four sets of four-view artwork derived from specific photographs are included to further enhance this book's appeal.

It is not the author's intention to provide a comprehensive development history of the various types of aircraft featured as, in most instances, such histories have been thoroughly

Hunter F.6 XG274 '71', of No.4 Flying Training School (FTS), RAF Valley, seen at Leconfield, Yorkshire, 27 July 1968. Delivered in January 1957, this aircraft served in turn with No.14 Squadron, No.229 OCU and finally No.4 FTS. Its final duties were as a ground-instructional airframe at Halton, Buckinghamshire, where it received the maintenance serial 8710M in November 1981; XG274/8710M was later preserved.
Chris Salter collection

documented elsewhere, especially so with the Hunter, Canberra and DH Vampire T.11; that said brief introductions to those aircraft are provided. The Vickers Valetta however has been awarded a little more attention as so little has ever been written about it, with only one published history to this author's knowledge.

Most of the images reproduced in this series, unless otherwise stated, are provided courtesy of the Newark Air Museum, located at Winthorpe, Nottinghamshire. The author would like to express his gratitude to the museums curator Mike Smith for the use of his valuable time, knowledge and resources as well as to other members of the museum staff for their courtesy and assistance over a period of many months. Grateful thanks are also extended to: Tony Buttler, Richard

Caruana, Mat Potulski (of Hawker Hunter Aviation Ltd), Chris Salter, Tony O'Toole, Simon Watson and to Doug Derry for the scores of hours he spent collating hundreds of photographs and negatives in preparation for this and other titles.

Authors note: Wherever possible dates and locations have been included based on information supplied with the images, often however, the information failed to survive the decades – whereas the images did.

Additionally, where possible an aircraft's delivery date, or date of first flight, or date that it was awaiting collection is provided. However, sources vary considerably with regard to such details.

Martin Derry, May 2010

Hawker Hunter FGA.9, XG156 'F', No.54 Squadron. The location and date is not specified although it most likely precedes September 1969, the date when the Squadron re-equipped with McDonnell Douglas Phantom FGR.2s with which it continued in its ground-attack role. Delivered as an F.6 on 27 November 1956, XG156 served with Nos.54 and 43 Squadrons prior to being converted to an FGA.9. Thereafter it was allocated to No.54

Squadron once more, following which it was transferred to No.229 Operational Conversion Unit, its final unit. On 9 October 1971, whilst operating from Gibraltar, XG156's undercarriage refused to lock down, however the pilot elected to attempt a landing but the aircraft struck a wall or similar obstruction and the pilot was killed.
Chris Salter collection

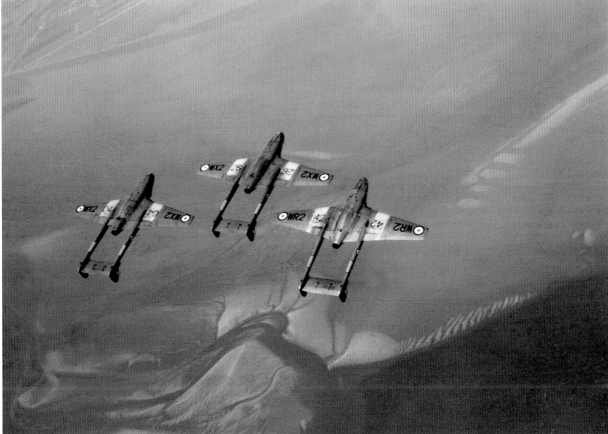

Top: *Not all Vampire trainers were two-seat examples, many single-seat Vampires were used for solo instruction following the students introduction to the T.11, hence their inclusion here outside the T.11 section. Having served with Nos.26 and 118 Squadrons, Vampire FB.5 VV486 was later allocated to No.8 FTS as seen here; it was scrapped in May 1959.* Newark Air Museum

Above: *Single-seat Vampire FB.9s were also used as witnessed here by WR242, WX204 and WX226 from the RAFC 'looping' over the littoral of eastern England. WX204 was struck off charge on 20th July 1959 and the other two were scrapped in September 1960. Vampire FB.5s and FB.9s used in the training role were often recorded as FB(T).5 and FB(T).9 respectively.* Tony Buttler collection

1   Vickers Valetta

During World War II, Britain's aircraft industry was, predictably, dominated by the need to develop and produce combat aircraft which in turn dictated that most transport aircraft would need to be obtained by other means, principally: those supplied by the USA, the adaptation of obsolete/obsolescent bombers and the impressment of suitable civil aircraft. There were, as ever, exceptions – the Avro York being one – which was designed and built specifically as a transport during the war years and epitomised perhaps by the VVIP York LV633, used by Winston Churchill and named '*Ascalon*' after St. George's lance.

Before the end of the war it had become clear that Britain would require civil freight and airliners in the immediate post-war years and that purpose designed machines would be more practical and cost effective than de-militarised bombers. In particular, a need was identified for a short-haul transport suitable for the European routes then envisaged and it was needed without delay! Vickers examined a number of projects from 1944 with a view to answering the Air Ministry's need and concluded that a civil development of their famous Wellington bomber might provide a suitable starting point. It did.

The resulting Vickers Viking incorporated a stressed-skin fuselage, with essentially, the Wellington's wing and to a lesser extent, elements of the Vickers Warwick too. From the outset it was intended that the Viking would feature a stressed-skin construction throughout in lieu of the fabric covered geodetic construction which characterised the Wellington. However, although the first 19 built were completed with stressed-skin fuselages, they received fabric covered geodetic wings and empennage, although eventually most of the 'geodetic' Vikings were retrospectively fitted with stressed-skin wings etcetera.

In the beginning. The Hercules powered Wellington formed the basis from which the Viking and Valetta were derived. Wellington MF628, seen here during the 1960s, was built as a B.X in 1944 and converted to a T.10 in March 1948 when the front turret was removed. Allocated to No.1 ANS in April 1949, by early 1950 it was painted overall High Speed Silver with yellow training bands applied. This aircraft later assisted and appeared in the film classic 'The Dam Busters' in 1954. MF628's last flight, and therefore the last flight of any Wellington, occurred on 24 January 1955 when it was flown to the Vickers airfield at Wisley, Surrey for eventual preservation. It now resides within the RAF Museum, Hendon.
Newark Air Museum

The Viking, as with particular marks of Wellington, was powered by two Bristol Hercules engines which also powered both the later Valetta and, later still, the Vickers Varsity, although the power output varied with the specific type of Hercules used. Of three prototypes, G-AGOK made the first ever Viking flight on 22 June 1945, piloted by 'Mutt' Summers. Ultimately, approximately 163 Vikings were built, the vast majority of which entered into airline service. However, several Vikings served with the Ministry of Supply (MoS) for a range of test or experimental purposes, including Viking VX618 which, having had its Hercules engines substituted for Rolls-Royce Nene jet engines, became the world's first all-jet transport aircraft to fly on 6 April 1948.

Several Vikings entered RAF service, with perhaps those of the King's (later the Queen's) Flight being the most obvious and included VL246 and VL247, which were both extensively modified and (possibly) designated as C(VVIP).2s. Other Vikings in RAF service were evaluated in an extensive series of trials to test the aircraft's suitability as a freighter, glider-tug, troop-transport, supply dropping and other roles, in an effort to find a replacement for the ubiquitous Douglas Dakota. The Viking proved very successful and as a

Viking 1B; despite the background clutter the physical link with the Valetta was very apparent. G-AJBT was first registered in June 1947 and obtained by British European Airways the following month. On 12 May 1965, G-AJBT's Permanent Withdrawal From Use was signed and the aircraft was subsequently scrapped. Presumably this image was obtained shortly after the latter date as it appears to be in a reasonable external condition and still has curtains in the cabin windows.
Newark Air Museum

Above: C.1 VW197, '197', date and location unknown. This aircraft was one of the few Valettas to survive in service long enough to receive Air Support Command titles in lieu of the earlier Transport Command titles displayed here. When this image was taken, VW197 was finished in Transport Command's then standard colour scheme of overall High Speed Silver with a white upper fuselage separated by a blue cheat-line. Later, this aircraft's silver paint was replaced by Light Aircraft Grey excepting the fin and rudder which were painted white. Following withdrawal VW197 was preserved for a time, although it was subsequently broken-up. Author's collection

Above right: C.1 VW197 once more, seen on 5 September 1962 at RAF Odiham whilst on the strength of the RAF College of Air Warfare. Author's collection

consequence a military Viking on order for the RAF, VL249, was duly completed as the prototype Valetta C.1; it first flew on 30 June 1947.

The Valetta C.1 differed from the Viking principally by employing a reinforced cabin floor capable of withstanding heavier loads and, by the provision of two large loading doors in the port rear fuselage. A smaller door was set within them for use as an exit for paratroopers or, as an access door for personnel. Inside the fuselage, lashing points, vehicle ramps, a loading winch or stretchers could be fitted according to need. Additionally, glider towing equipment could be fitted if required. This was a role still deemed relevant at that time and for which the Valetta was fitted with a heavy metal structure in the rear fuselage to which the towing hook

and release gear was connected. Although the prototype and several production C.1s had a faired tail cone fitted, most C.1s featured a blunt truncated rear end which terminated slightly aft of the rudder. In the troop transport role, the Valetta was able to accommodate 34 fully equipped soldiers and their equipment, or 20 stretcher cases plus two medical orderlies, or 20 paratroopers with their equipment stowed within a maximum of nine 350lb containers carried externally below the fuselage.

The first flight of a production Valetta (VL262) occurred in January 1948 and the first recipient was No.240 OCU, which began to receive them later that year. The OCU had formed at North Luffenham, Rutland, on 5 January 1948 with 41 Dakotas assigned to training crews for the RAF's medium-range transport squadrons; thus, with the arrival of the first Valettas, the way was paved for that aircraft's introduction to squadron service and the eventual displacement of the Dakota.

In service the Valetta C.1 quickly equipped, or partially equipped, several squadrons principally as a transport aircraft within Transport Command and its middle and far eastern equivalents, but not exclusively so; No.683 Squadron for example, operated in the Middle East as a survey unit from November 1950 equipped with Lancaster PR.1s and Valetta's VW192, VX498, VX557.

Those squadrons known to have received C.1s were: Number's 30, 48, 52, 70, 78, 84, 110, 114, 115, 167, 187, 204, 216, 233, 622 and 683, plus No.1312 Flight which had reformed on 14 September 1954 with Handley Page Hastings, supplemented by Valettas from 1955 until disbanded in April 1957. Additionally, No.173 and No.205 Squadrons may also have been equipped with the C.1, although sources conflict as to whether or not this was so! Of interest was No.622 Squadron; it became the only transport squadron within the Royal Auxiliary Air Force when reformed in December 1950. In addition to the squadrons listed, it should be noted that the Valetta served with a host of RAF training, evaluation, research, communication and conversion units and with the MoS.

Below: *C.1 WD159, 'O'. Delivered on 6 October 1950, this aircraft was first issued to No.52 Squadron in Malaya in 1951, the cabin titles read 'Far East Transport Wing'. This was an organisation formed on 1 January 1952, at Changi, Singapore, to control the efforts of Nos.48, 52 and 110 Squadrons. Additionally, the Wing boasted two Valetta C.1s for 'sky shouting' purposes i.e. they were fitted with loud speakers. This image of WD159 was taken at USAF Clark Field, in the Philippines.* Newark Air Museum

Left: *Towards the end of its flying career, WD159 'Z' appears in very different guise to the previous photograph. Seen at Wyton on 14 September 1963, WD159 was serving with either the CNCS or CATCS which were the last two flying units to which it was allocated. On 3 September 1964, this Valetta became 7858M at Colerne, later becoming an exhibit. With the closure of the museum, 7858M went to Hereford in March 1976 for use by the SAS Regiment and (apparently) blown up towards the end of 1977.* Newark Air Museum

C.1 WJ491, seen at A&AEE Boscombe Down 18 March 1971. Delivered in May 1951, this Valetta was first allocated to the TRE before joining the A&AEE in 1961. Thereafter, WJ491 remained with the latter unit until March 1972, following which it was flown to RAF Gatow, Berlin, where it was struck off charge the following month and used for fire practice. It is presumed that this was the last Valetta ever to have flown (excluding 'flights' as an underslung load). The yellow disc aft of the cockpit is the A&AEE Motif extracted from the A&AEE Badge and shows two gauntlets clasped, intersected by an arrow.
Author's collection

An anonymous Valetta C.1 or C.2, (both marks featured the large loading doors shown here to advantage), date and location unknown. This aircraft is devoid of any visible identification although doubtless its serial or maintenance number is obscured by the open door!
Author's collection

C.2 VX577, date and location unknown. This Valetta served with a host of units during its service having been delivered from Vickers in February 1950 and issued to No.24 Squadron shortly thereafter. In 1968, at the end of its active service, it was placed in storage until mid-January 1969 when it was bought for preservation. At a later date VX577 was donated to the North East Aircraft Museum near Sunderland and destroyed there following an arson attack in January 1997.
Author's collection

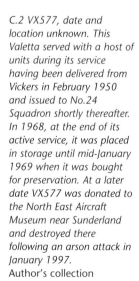

Valetta C.1s, (nicknamed 'Pig' in RAF service) were allocated the following serial numbers: VL249 (prototype), VL262-VL282, VW140-165, VW180-VW206, VW802-VW851, VW855-VW864, VX483-VX485, VX490-VX499, VX506-VX515, VX521-VX530, VX537-VX546, VX555-VX563, WD157-WD171, WJ491-WJ499. A total of 211 C.1s including the prototype. Note: VX500 was deleted from the production contract and delivered to the Royal Swedish Air Force. Orders for serials WD172-WD197 and WD244-WD275 were cancelled.

The Valetta C.2 was built as a VIP aircraft and externally at least appeared identical to those C.1s fitted with a (VX576), as well as several other units e.g. the Aden Communication Flight, the Ferry Support Squadron and the RAF Flying College (RAFFC) to name but a few.

Valetta C.2 serial numbers were: VX571-VX580, WJ504. 11 in total.

The final production variant, the Valetta T.3, (nicknamed 'Inverted Sow') was a flying classroom equipped for a maximum of 10 student navigators and was externally identified by a row of six dorsal astrodomes; hence its nickname. Individual T.3s were issued, as required, to squadrons already equipped with the Valetta, known examples being: No.70 (WJ462 & WJ481), No.84 (WG257,

An unidentified C.2, date and location unknown. The black rectangle situated towards the tip of the nose bears four stars, presumably denoting this aircraft to be the steed of a very high ranking officer or official. Newark Air Museum

pointed tail cone. Internally, at least one (WJ504), or perhaps all of the C.2s carried an extra 116 gallons of fuel located in Viking-type nacelle saddle tanks, whilst a 'plush' cabin interior was fitted with accommodation for nine to fifteen VIPs. The A&AEE at Boscombe Down didn't heap much praise upon the interior seating of the C.2, they merely stated that the seats were less uncomfortable than those in a C.1!

The Valetta C.2 is known to have served with the following squadrons: No.24 (VX576 & VX577), No.30 (VX574, VX576, VX577 & WJ504), No.70 (VX572 & VX577), No.84 (VX579), No.114 (VX580) and No.233 WJ466 & WJ481), No.114 (WJ464) and No.115 (VX564). Far more relevant however was the T.3's service with the various training units, examples being: the Air Electronics School (AES), Nos. 1, 2, 3, 5, & 6 Air Navigation Schools (ANS), No.228 & 238 OCUs, the RAF College (RAFC) and RAFFC.

Valetta T.3 serial numbers were: VX564 (prototype), WG256-WG267, WJ461-WJ487. 40 in total.

The Valetta T.4 was used for radar training and incorporated a radar in a distinctively extended nose. Eighteen T.4s were procured; all were converted from the Valetta T.3 and allocated principally to No.2 ANS and 228 OCU.

Above: T.3 WG257 'D', Cranwell, Lincolnshire, 20 January 1962.
Delivered in August 1950, this aircraft served with the CSDE,
No.84 Squadron, RAFC (twice), MoA and No.2 ANS before being
allocated the maintenance serial 7999M in November 1967. This
image shows WG257 during one of its two periods with the RAFC
at Cranwell, indicated by the characteristic blue fuselage band as
applied to many of the College's aircraft, accompanied here with
spinner caps of the same colour. The wing and engine behind
WG237 belong to a Varsity. Newark Air Museum

Below: T.3 WG262 'C', Waddington, Lincolnshire, September
1959. Delivered in October 1951, this Valetta served with No.2
ANS, the RRE, then No.2 ANS once more. It was struck off charge
on 18 August 1961, at No.71 MU Bicester, Oxfordshire.
Newark Air Museum

T.3 airframes converted to T.4 were: WG256, WG263, WG267, WJ464-WJ467, WJ469, WJ471-WJ473, WJ475, WJ477, WJ482, WJ483, WJ485, WJ486, WJ487. 18 in total.

It would appear that 75 Valettas were written off following accidents, the first being VW160 on 28 November 1949 at RAF Deversoir, Egypt, following an engine failure at take-off. The last appears to have occurred on 16 December 1964 when VW182 crashed whilst allocated to No.52 Squadron. The following is a list of Valetta accidents in which fatalities were incurred amongst passengers or crew:

18/02/51 C.1 VX514, RAFFC; lost power in blizzard, force-landed near Stockholm, Sweden: 1 fatality.

02/05/51 C.1 VW156, 78 Sqn; parachute fouled tailplane, a/c crashed near Fayid, Egypt: 8 fatalities.

12/07/51 C.1 VW194, 242 OCU; crashed near Lyneham, Wilts, cause not known: 10 fatalities.

17/09/51 C.1 VW813, 78 Sqn; outer wing broke off in turbulence, near Loka, Sudan: 4 fatalities.

02/08/52 C.1 VX540, 52 Sqn; stalled (?) during supply drop, near Kuala Lumpur, Malaya: 7 fatalities.

19/08/52 C.1 VL266, ETPS; crashed near RAF Odiham, Hants: 2 fatalities.

19/08/52 C.1 VX559, 30 Sqn; flew into ground after night take-off, near RAF Benson, Oxon: 3 fatalities.

Two images of T.3 WG264 'N-H', over flying RAF Cranwell, possibly during 1963. The letter 'N' was Cranwell's identifying letter for both the Valetta and Varsity from approximately 1956, whilst 'H' was this aircraft's individual identifying letter. WG264 was delivered in November 1951 and operated in turn by Nos.5, 6 and 1 ANS, prior to being allocated to the RAFC. It was struck off charge in July 1968 and subsequently burnt at Abingdon.
Newark Air Museum

T.3 WJ481 'N-A', date and location unknown. Delivered in June 1952, this aircraft survived until June 1968 when it was struck off charge and later burnt for fire fighting practice at Fairford, Gloucestershire. During its active career, WJ481 had served with Nos.78 and 84 Squadrons prior to joining the RAFC with whom this aircraft was serving when this photograph was taken, by which point the aircraft's colour scheme seemed very 'tired'. Newark Air Museum

15/01/53 C.1 VX562, Malta CS; collided with Lancaster GR3, Italy: 19 fatalities (plus 7 crew in Lancaster)

07/05/53 T.3 WG258, 1 ANS; into sea near Hartland Point, North Devon: 10 fatalities.

17/05/53 C.1 VW810, 70 Sqn; controls jammed, force-landed and caught fire, Luqa, Malta: 2 fatalities.

26/09/53 C.1 WD164, 48 Sqn; flew into high ground, NW of Bertam, Malaya: 8 fatalities.

11/11/53 C.1 VX490, 48 Sqn; presumed to have broken up in storm near Singapore Island: 7 fatalities.

16/12/53 C.1 VX575, Malta CF; over speeding prop, a/c crash-landed near Luqa, Malta: 1 fatality.

06/01/54 T.3 WJ474, 2 ANS; hit tree near Aldbury, Herts: 16 fatalities.

20/01/54 C.1 VL282, 30 Sqn; near Lyneham: 1 fatality.

21/02/54 C.1 WJ494, Far East Transport Wing; lost height, RAF Changi, Singapore: 3 fatalities.

23/02/54 C.1 WD160, Far East Transport Wing; struck Mt Ophir, south of Gemas, Malaya: 4 fatalities.

02/04/54 C.1 VW205, 216 Sqn; struck mountain, Jebel al Lawz, Saudi Arabia: 3 fatalities.

02/03/56 C.1 VW861, 48 Sqn; struck trees, Cameron Highlands, Malaya: 7 fatalities.

15/06/56 C.1 VX521, 110 Sqn; stalled near Ipoh, Malaya: 9 fatalities.

23/11/56 C.1 VX525, 48 Sqn; stalled during supply drop, Cameron Highlands: 7 fatalities.

17/04/57 C.1 VW832, 84 Sqn; wing broke off in turbulence, near Aqaba, Jordan: 27 fatalities.

22/08/57 C.1 VX491, 110 Sqn; flew into hill, Perak, Malaya: 3 fatalities.

28/08/62 T.3 WJ480, 2 ANS; asymmetric overshoot, crashed 5 miles NW of Chippenham, Wilts: 3 fatalities.

Additionally, the following were all written off in non-fatal accidents, although injuries must have been suffered by Valetta occupants on occasion. (All serials refer to C.1s, unless otherwise stated).

VL271, VL279, VW140, VW143, VW151, VW153, VW160, VW164, VW165, VW180, VW182, VW183, VW184, VW185, VW187, VW203, VW204, VW206, VW803, VW804, VW805, VW812, VW817, VW823, VW824, VW827, VW828, VW833, VW834, VW840, VW845, VW846, VW863, VX483, VX492, VX497, VX498, VX499, VX507, VX515, VX537, VX538, VX544, VX557, VX571(C.2), WD163, WD165, WD170, WG265(T.3), WJ467(T.4), WJ470(T.3).

The type remained in service in its various roles and ever-diminishing quantities until the late-1960s, although all remaining VL serialled Valettas had been removed from flying duties by late 1959. On 1 August 1967, RAF Transport Command was re-titled RAF Support Command and a handful of Valettas survived long enough to have the new title applied to their fuselages in lieu of the former; VW197 was one such example. By 1969 it would appear that just two flyable specimens were left in the RAF, although both VW847 and VW856 had been struck off by the middle of the year and scrapped. The A&AEE however, retained their own 'pet' Valetta WJ491 for transport duties until March 1972, thus becoming, presumably, the last Valetta to fly. Additionally, a few Valetta's served on as ground instructional airframes once their respective flying careers were over; a known example being WD159 which, having received the maintenance serial 7858M, served at RAF Colerne, Wiltshire from September 1964. It later became an exhibit in the museum located there until 1975 when, unfortunately, the RAF Colerne Station Museum was closed and WD159/7858M disposed of.

In preservation, at least five of the species existed – for a time. WD159/7858M has already been mentioned, in addition C.1 VW197 was struck off charge on 3 January 1969 and 'preserved', but was broken-up at a later date. For a while it was thought that the cockpit section had survived at 'Aeroventure', Doncaster; however, recent research suggests that the museum's cockpit section may have in fact come from T.3 WJ476. The remaining three aircraft were all C.2s: VX573, VX577 and VX580. VX573 is located at the RAF Museum, Cosford and VX580 at the Norfolk & Suffolk Aviation Museum, Flixton, Suffolk. VX577 was destroyed in an arson attack in 1997.

Three Valetta T.3s belonging to the RAFC at Cranwell, date not known. All three show variations in their respective colour schemes, 'N-A', WJ481 being closest to the camera. The centre aircraft, 'N-G', does not have a white upper fuselage, whereas the other two do! Newark Air Museum

WJ481 'N-A' once more. By the time that this image was taken, 'N-A' had received a considerable amount of external attention and makes a pleasing contrast in comparison with the earlier photographs.
Newark Air Museum

The Valetta had a wing-span of 89ft 3ins and a length (excluding T.4) of 65ft 2ins, (62ft 11 ins with C.1 truncated tail cone). It was powered by two Bristol Hercules 230 engines each with a power output of 1,975 hp at take-off, and could achieve a service ceiling of 22,000ft with a top speed of approximately 259mph at 10,000ft.

The Valetta C.1's empty weight was a little under 25,000lb with an all-up weight of 36,500lbs. The C.1 had a maximum range of 1,410 miles decreasing significantly depending upon the payload carried; i.e. approximately 350 miles when carrying 34 troops. Its maximum payload was 8,000lb.

Opposite top: T.3 'N-G' (G being the individual code), RAFC. Identity, date and location unknown. The loading doors fitted to the C.1 and C.2 were omitted in the T.3, which was used for the training of navigators who required the use of the several astrodomes so well defined in this image; hence the soubriquet,' inverted sow'. Newark Air Museum

Opposite bottom: T.4 WG256 'S', date and location unknown. Delivered as a T.3 in March 1951, WG256 was one of 18 Valetta T.3s modified to T.4 standard and easily identified by their characteristic nose extension which incorporated a radar scanner. Used to train navigators in the use of airborne radar, five of the T.3s astrodomes were removed, the trainees needing only to look at their screens as they pursued suitable targets about the British skies. Following conversion, this aircraft was operated by a number of units including No.228 OCU and No.2 ANS until, by early 1967, it had been struck off charge and subsequently expired on the fire dump at RAF Wyton. Author's collection

Vickers Valetta T.3, WG264 'N-H', from RAF College, Cranwell.
For further details please refer to page 17. Not to scale.

2   Hawker Hunter

Above: *Hawker P.1052 VX279, photographed in 1949 or 1950. In no sense a Hunter nor even a prototype, this and sister P.1052, VX272 were produced to gain knowledge in the field of high-subsonic flight, and in that respect at least, the information and experience obtained proved useful to the later Hunter programme, hence the tentative inclusion of this image. VX279 is shown in its original form painted Duck Egg Green overall; Hawker's 'house' colour for prototype aircraft. Flown for the first time on 13 April 1949, the aircraft displays its original tailplane and bifurcated jet pipe which were retained until April 1950, from which date the aircraft was taken in hand to be rebuilt. The rebuilding was restricted to the area aft of the rear engine bay and featured a straight-through Supermarine Attacker-type jet pipe and swept variable incidence tailplane, the combination of which conferred a much sleeker appearance. In its refined form, VX279 was designated P.1081 and first flew as such on 19 June 1950, retaining its original 5,000lb s.t (static thrust) Rolls-Royce Nene engine. The P.1081 conducted various flight tests which revealed subtle performance improvements over the P.1052 prior to it crashing on 3 April 1951, killing the pilot Squadron Leader T S Wade.* Newark Air Museum

The Hawker Hunter was designed as a single-seat, swept-wing, high-subsonic day interceptor fighter for the Royal Air Force. It was required to supersede the existing day fighters operated by RAF Fighter Command; principally the Gloster Meteor F.8 as well as two (Canadair-built) North American F-86 Sabre units, operated by Nos.66 and 92 Squadrons, based at Linton-on-Ouse, Yorkshire. Additionally, Hunters were also required as the essential element for the modernisation of the RAF's fighter squadrons in West Germany, where they would replace existing day-fighter types including ten squadrons of (stop-gap) Sabres, obtained as aid from the USA. The first unit to receive the Sabre had been No.67 Squadron at Wildenrath in March 1953 and Sabres remained the only RAF fighter, prior to the Hunter's arrival, capable of dealing with Soviet Mig-15 fighters based, in quantity, in the German Democratic Republic, i.e. East Germany.

Five marks of new-build single-seat Hunters entered RAF service at home and abroad, (omitting later conversions of existing marks e.g. FGA.9, FR.10 etcetera) they were: F.1, F.2, F.4, F.5 and F.6. The new British interceptor's performance transformed the RAF's day-fighter squadrons from the mid-1950s, despite initially being beset by a host of problems which included that enduring characteristic of certain British fighters; an appalling lack of endurance. The various faults were overcome in due course, aided by the utilisation of approximately 20 early production F.1s, virtually as prototypes – the Hunter development programme having only allowed for three true prototypes, far

too few given the innovative design of the new type. Included amongst the innovations were the inclusion of gun-ranging radar, four nose-mounted 30mm ADEN revolver cannon which, although seemingly anachronistic today, at the time, prior to the advent of air-to-air missiles, offered unparalleled firepower. Further, these weapons were mounted in a detachable ventral gun-pack that contained the breeches of the four cannon and their ammunition, allowing the pack to be quickly removed on landing and replaced with a pre-loaded unit. This feature permitted a rapid rearming and turn-around time, the latter enhanced in later marks of Hunter by the important inclusion of a

Left: *Hunter F.5 WP126/7569M, post July 1965, Cranwell, Lincolnshire. Certainly not the most flattering image of an elegant aircraft but, alphanumerically at least, it is the earliest serial number to appear in this section. Delivered on 16 May 1955, this aircraft was operated in turn by Nos.1, 34 and 208 Squadrons before receiving the maintenance serial 7569M on 4 June 1958. By 12 July 1965 it was in use at Cranwell for fire training. Despite extensive burning, the wing tips had remained untouched by fire when these images were obtained and were still painted white; a surviving indication perhaps of WP126's earlier, albeit brief service with No.208 Squadron. The hulk was scrapped at Cranwell North in 1977.*
Both Newark Air Museum

Left: *Hunter F.5, possibly WP183 'V', No.56 Squadron circa 1956. This image exemplifies how aerodynamically clean the Hunter was in its near original form when devoid of underwing tanks or cartridge link collectors for its cannon. This aircraft is seen displaying No.56 Squadron's traditional red and white checks on the nose either side of the phoenix Emblem extracted from the Squadron Badge. Additionally, red and white checks were applied to each wing tip. This unit operated the F.5 from May 1955 until November 1958 when they were replaced by the F.6. Delivered 30 June 1955, WP183 served only with this unit before going to the MoS in February 1959.* Tony Buttler collection

Opposite top: *Hunter F.1 WT594 'U', No.43 Squadron, circa 1955. Based at Leuchars, Fife, this unit was the first to introduce the Hunter F.1 into operational squadron service in July 1954. WT594 was first flown in July 1955 and allocated to No.222 Squadron in early December 1954, prior to being reallocated to No.43 Squadron just two weeks later. The aircraft is seen in company with F.1's WT622/G, fitted with link collectors and WT641/T. All display the Squadron's black and white chequered markings which, in the case of WT622, shows evidence of the disfigurement caused to them by engine cooling and exhaust stains. Commonly, Hunter units frequently resolved this problem by moving their 'bars' higher up the fuselage sides, or onto the nose section. WT594 later went on to serve with the Day Fighter Leaders School (DFLS), a component of the CFE, in 1954, and No.229 OCU before being sold for scrap in April 1958. WT622 later went to No.229 OCU before receiving the maintenance serial 7562M in November 1957. WT641 served with the DFLS and No.229 OCU before becoming 7529M, also in November 1957.* Tony Buttler collection

Opposite bottom: *Hunter F.1 WT612/7496M, on 10 August 1964, Yatesbury, Wiltshire. First flown in July 1954, this aircraft was used to trial the Rolls-Royce Avon 115 engine before it was allocated to the A&AEE at Boscombe Down, Wiltshire, where it arrived on 5 June 1956. Its function there initially was to conduct gun-firing trials, it having been discovered that Hunters fitted with the Avon 115 experienced less engine surge problems than those fitted with earlier types of Avon. WT612 also trialled an Avon 121 installation in combination with gun-firing tests and proved able to fire its weapons satisfactorily up to an altitude of 48,000 ft. Hunters fitted with the Avon 113 were restricted to firing their guns below 25,000ft, an unacceptable limitation. This aircraft never joined an RAF Squadron or flying unit, becoming a ground instructional airframe instead and received the maintenance serial 7496M in November 1957. WT612 was retained in this role until 1984. Part of its service was spent with No.2 Radio School, Yatesbury, until the unit disbanded on 31 October 1965. WT612 survived into preservation and now resides at Henlow, Bedfordshire.*
Newark Air Museum

single point, pressure input, refuelling system. Their combination, amongst other considerations allowed the Hunter to be readied between sorties in an unprecedented seven or eight minutes if required, the relevance of which, in a Cold War climate, remains self evident.

That the Hunter proved to be a success in British and foreign service there can be little doubt and in its primary role as a fighter, at home and abroad, the F.1 to F.6 (the Mk 3 did not enter service) served with numerous RAF frontline squadrons. In the United Kingdom, the English Electric Lightning was introduced into squadron service from mid-1960 and commenced its replacement of the Hunter as the RAF's premier air defence interceptor fighter, a process completed by April 1963, for those squadrons which were not otherwise axed. (Hunter FGA.9s of Nos.1 and 54 Squadrons remained available in the UK throughout the 1960s as dedicated ground-attack units.) The Hunter however was destined to serve Britain's military in a host of other roles for many decades, albeit in diminishing quantities and continued to serve a number of foreign air forces with great longevity too. In fact as recently as 2008, in the Lebanon, a few Hunters were brought out of

storage with the intention of returning them to limited operational service.

Improbably, despite the Hunter's 'final' retirement from British military service several years ago, two ex-Swiss Mk.58 Hunters were allocated military serials ZZ190 and ZZ191 in late 2006 and leased to provide training support for the RAF and RN as necessary. Additionally, two further Hunters re-entered the military register and assumed their original serials, they were: T.8B XF995 in 2007 and T.8C XF994 in early 2010. Since the summer of 2009, each has had the legend 'Royal Navy' applied to their rear fuselage. In March 2010, a third ex-Swiss Mk.58 Hunter was entered onto the military register as ZZ194; further examples of Mk.58 Hunters are expected to join the others in the foreseeable future. All are owned by Hawker Hunter Aviation Ltd, an MoD approved and regulated company based at Scampton, Lincolnshire, where HHA Ltd maintains further airworthy Hunters and other ex-military jets to assist the UK's armed forces and other defence agencies as required.

In Canada, a company called 'Northern Lights Combat Air Support' also maintain and operate a quantity of Hunters for similar purposes.

Hunter T.7 WV253 '24', date and location not known, formerly an F.4. First flown on 29 April 1955, this aircraft was first operated by the Radar Research Establishment (RRE) followed by 4 Squadron prior to its conversion to a T.7. Following the conversion, this aircraft was operated by the Empire Test Pilots School (ETPS), as seen here; their Unit Badge is fully reproduced on the aircraft's nose bordered by the words 'Empire Test Pilots School'. The scroll at the foot of the Badge bears the legend 'Learn To Test - Test To Learn'. WV253 spun into the sea off Lyme Regis, Dorset on 15 July 1968.
Newark Air Museum

SERIAL NUMBER ALLOCATIONS

The serial numbers of those Hunters delivered into *British* service are listed below and refer to the aircraft as completed. It should be noted that a large number of aircraft were later modified and redesignated, (F.6 to FGA.9 for instance), whilst others, later in life were returned to the manufacturer and converted into two-seat training aircraft. All but a very few retained their original serial number whilst in British service.

Prototypes

The first Hunter to fly was prototype WB188, (designated P.1067 by the manufacturer) on 20 July 1951 in the hands of Squadron Leader Neville Duke. The second prototype was WB195 first flown on 5 May 1952 and was representative of the later production Hunter F.1s as it incorporated a tail buffet fairing, gun ranging radar and cannon armament all of which WB188 lacked. Both aircraft were fitted with variants of the Rolls-Royce Avon engine, whilst the third prototype, WB202, was fitted with an Armstrong-Siddeley Sapphire engine and full armament to become, in effect, the prototype Hunter F.2. It flew for the first time on 30 November 1952. The Sapphire engine was confined to the F.2 and F.5, all other production Hunter variants received Avon engines of various marks and power output.

F.1

Hunter F.1 serial numbers comprised: WT555-WT595, WT611-WT660, WT679-WT700, WW599-WW610, WW632-WW645. WT555 became the first production Hunter to fly on 16 May 1953.The first unit to receive production Hunters was the Air Fighting Development Squadron (AFDS) within the Central Fighter Establishment (CFE) in July 1954. F.1s served with Nos.43, 54, 222 and 247 Squadrons.

F.2

Hunter F.2 serials comprised: WN888-WN921, WN943-WN953. They were operated by Nos.257 and 263 Squadrons, the former being the first to equip with the F.2 in September 1954.

Mark 3

The solitary Mark 3 was in fact prototype WB188 which, modified and redesignated, was used to trial a reheat equipped Avon engine. This aircraft was subsequently flown by Neville Duke in an attempt to capture the world speed record which was accomplished on 7 September 1953, attaining a world absolute speed record of 726.6mph.

F.4

Hunter F.4 serials comprised: WT701-WT723, WT734-WT780, WT795-WT811, WV253-WV281, WV314-WV334, WV363-WV412, WW589-WW591, WW646-665, XE657-XE689, XE702-XE718, XF289-XF324, XF357-XF370, XF932-XF953, XF967-XF999, XG341and XG342. The F.4 was allocated to the following squadrons: Nos.3, 4, 14, 20, 26, 43, 54, 66, 67, 71, 74, 92, 93, 98, 111, 112, 118, 130, 222, 234, 245 and 247.

F.5

Hunter F.5 serials comprised: WN954-WN992, WP101-WP150, WP179-WP194. The F.5 was allocated to the following squadrons: Nos.1, 34, 41, 56, 208, 257 and 263.

F.6

Hunter F.6 serials comprised: WW592-WW598, XE526-XE561, XE579-XE628, XE643-XE656, XF373-XF389, XF414-XF463, XF495-XF527, XF833 (the latter became the prototype F.6 which, incidentally, utilised sections of the abandoned P.1083 supersonic Hunter ex-WN470), XG127-XG137, XG150-XG172, XG185-XG211, XG225-XG239, XG251-XG274, XG289-XG298, XJ632-XJ646, XJ673-XJ695, XJ712-XJ718, XK136-XK156 (of which XK143-XK147 and XK152-XK156 were delivered to the RAF in August and September 1957, then stored at maintenance units prior to being passed to Iraq the following December). XK157-XK176 and XK213-XK224 did not enter British service, going directly to the Indian Air Force on completion. The F.6 was allocated to the following squadrons: Nos.1, 4, 14, 19, 20, 26, 43, 54, 56, 63, 65, 66, 74, 92, 93, 111, 118 (possibly!), 208, 247 and 263.

T.7

New-build Hunter T.7 serials comprised: XJ615 and XJ627 (for Ministry of Aviation), XL563-XL579, XL583, XL586, XL587, XL591-XL597, XL600, XL601, XL605 (sold to Saudi Arabia in 1966 and returned to the RAF in 1974 as XX467) and XL609-XL623, (XL620 sold to Saudi Arabia in 1966 and returned to the RAF in 1974 as XX466). Known conversions to T.7 from single-seat F.4s include WV253, WV318, WV372, WV383, XF310 and XF321. Most RAF Hunter squadrons received at least one T.7 following the type's introduction to service from 1958, as well as training and support units.

T.7A

Four new-build T.7s were subsequently converted to T.7A standard by incorporating TACAN (TACtical Air Navigation) and other new flight instrumentation systems. In addition WV318 was also converted to a T.7A.

T.8

New-build Hunter T.8 serials comprised: XL580-XL582, XL584, XL585, XL598, XL599, XL602-XL604. All had been ordered as T.7s for the RAF but were transferred to the Admiralty for the Fleet Air Arm (FAA). Additionally, 31 or 32 F.4s were converted to T.8, T.8B or T.8C standard. (Sources vary regarding the quantity; perhaps F.4 WW664, by becoming both the T.8 prototype and later the T.8B prototype, created some confusion)

T.8B and T.8C

The T.8B and T.8C introduced TACAN equipment to the Service, with additional instrumentation being fitted to the T.8B – but not the T.8C. All were converted from F.4 airframes. T.8B XF995 (G-BZSF) re-joined the military register in 2007, followed by T.8C XF994 (G-CGHU) in 2010.

T.8M

XL580, XL602 and XL603 were fitted with Blue Fox radar both for the trials of, and later the training of Sea Harrier FRS.1 pilots.

FGA.9

128 Hunter F.6s were converted to become dedicated ground-attack aircraft and were redesignated FGA.9 (Fighter Ground Attack), including 36 which were converted initially to an interim FGA.9 standard (sometimes designated F.6A), before being further modified to the full FGA.9 specification – presuming that all 36 survived to receive the further upgrade! FGA.9s were allocated to the following squadrons: Nos.1, 4, 8, 20, 28, 43, 45, 54, 58 and 208.

FR.10

Either 32 or 33 Hunter F.6s were converted to the Fighter Reconnaissance (FR) role to become the Hunter FR.10. They were allocated to the following squadrons: Nos.2, 4 and 8. A number also equipped No.1417 (Fighter Reconnaissance) Flight at Khormaksar, Aden.

GA.11 and PR.11

40 surplus F.4s were converted to perform a tactical weapons training role for the Royal Navy designated GA.11. Their guns and associated equipment were removed and gun ports faired over and many were fitted with a Harley light at the tip of the nose to assist with optical tracking. A small number of GA.11s received a camera-nose installation and were (sometimes) referred to as the PR.11.

Mark 12

XE531 was the only example of its type and was a converted F.6 (later FGA.9). It was ordered for the RAE.

Mark 58

Two ex-Swiss Hunters of this mark entered the British military register as ZZ190 (J-4066/G-HHAE) and ZZ191 (J-4058/G-HHAD) in December 2006, followed by ZZ194 (J-4021/G-HHAC) in March 2010. Further examples of this variant may well be added in the future.

The precise quantity of Hunter airframes completed varies somewhat according to source but the figure of 1,972 seems to be widely accepted, almost 400 of which were later remanufactured to serve in other roles or with other countries.

Opposite top: *WV253 '24', September 1965, location not known. Subtle variations exist when this image of WV253 is compared to that on page 28. In this, the Unit Badge is superimposed on a white rectangular background and the under-wing tanks have received a black nose cap and horizontal stripe to match those on the aircraft's nose.* Newark Air Museum

Opposite centre: *Hunter FR.10 WW596 'N', No.2 Squadron, September 1961, Waddington, Lincolnshire. Formerly an F.6 first flown on 10 October 1955. Following delivery to the RAF this aircraft was placed at the disposal of the Metropolitan Sector Operations Centre of RAF Fighter Command which was located in a bunker deep underground at Kelvedon Hatch, Essex, intended to be proof against a near-miss by a 20 kiloton nuclear weapon. WW596 was next allocated to the Day Fighter Combat Squadron which had formed on 15 March 1958, within the Fighter Combat School, Central Fighter Establishment at West Raynham, Norfolk. In October 1959, it was returned to the manufacturer, converted to an FR.10 and returned to service in March 1961 to be later issued in turn to No.2 Squadron, 229 OCU and No.2 Squadron once again. By 3 March 1971 WW596 had been sold back to the manufacturer for re-sale to the Indian Air Force (IAF). In common with several Hunter-equipped units that displayed their squadron colours on either side of the fuselage roundel, No.2 Squadron's colours were applied relatively high, their bottom edge parallel with the centre of the roundel.* Newark Air Museum

Opposite bottom: *Hunter F.6 WW598. A member of the first F.6 production batch, this aircraft first flew on the last day of 1955, but was never operated by the RAF; instead it was first allocated to the RRE for missile trials after being fitted with a radar. It later joined the 'Aero Flight' at RAE Bedford having received at some point the overall blue colour scheme illustrated here. Later, WW598 participated in the TSR2 programme during which it was painted white, and ultimately was operated by the RAE at Llanbedr, Merionethshire. In May 1974 it was sold to Hawker Siddeley, refurbished, and subsequently delivered to the Lebanese Air Force. Unfortunately, neither a date or location has been supplied with either image reproduced here and on page 32, although the presence of mountains and a Meteor U.16/D.16 suggests perhaps Llanbedr. The words AERO FLIGHT appear in white on the aircraft's nose, below which and within the white cheat line the words RAE BEDFORD have been applied in red.* Newark Air Museum

Left: In the air it can be seen that although an F.6, WW598, in common with other early examples of this mark, is devoid of the distinctive 'dog-tooth' or more properly the wing leading-edge extensions that was a characteristic of later F.6s. Newark Air Museum

Below: Hunter Mk.12 XE531, Finningley, Yorkshire, 19 September 1964. Built as an F.6 this aircraft first flew in January 1956 and was subsequently converted to FGA.9 standard following which, during 1961/62, it was once again converted; this time to become a two-seat research aircraft for the RAE. Designated Mk.12, XE531 was the sole example of its type and was first flown in this form on 23 October 1962 and arrived at Farnborough in February 1963. In this image a distinctive bulge is visible on the upper surface of the nose which is believed to have housed an early example of a head-up display (HUD) system which was then under development. Ultimately the HUD equipment was removed and many later photographs of XE531 show that the bulge was removed also.

Following an extensive trials career, which included the testing of an early fly-by-wire system, the Mk.12 crashed following an engine explosion during take-off at Farnborough on 17 March 1982. XE531 was easily identified by virtue of its verdant colour scheme with white upper fuselage and vertical tail surfaces. The RAE's Badge appears below the cockpit as does the legend Royal Aircraft Establishment. Newark Air Museum

Opposite top: *Hunter F.6 XF375, Benson, Oxfordshire, autumn 1969. Delivered in August 1955, this aircraft was retained by the MoS, then, following periods with various aircraft manufacturers, it was allocated to the ETPS in 1963. By 1976 XF375 was with the RAE at Farnborough before going to the Royal Air Force College Cranwell Engineering Flight, as 8736M. It was subsequently sold into preservation.* Chris Salter collection

Opposite centre: *Hunter F.6 XF384 '72', No.4 Flying Training School (FTS), an undated image taken at Upper Heyford, Oxfordshire. Delivered in August 1956, this aircraft served operationally with a number of squadrons prior to joining the DFLS and Day Fighter Combat Squadron (DFCS). The DFLS disbanded on 15 March 1958 becoming the DFCS on the same day within the Fighter Combat School, itself a component of the CFE at West Raynham, Norfolk. XF384 went on to serve with No.229 OCU and later No.4 FTS at Valley in Wales. It was written-off following a mid-air collision with F.6 XF387 in which both pilots and aircraft were lost, the latter aircraft crashing into caravans in which one civilian was killed and others injured.* Chris Salter collection

Opposite bottom: *Hunter F.6 XF386 '33', No.4 FTS, August 1969. Delivered in August 1956, this aircraft served with Nos.66, 92, 63 and 65 Squadrons, 229 OCU and No.4 FTS. its final flying duties were with the Laarbruch Station Flight, West Germany, when, following the temporary grounding of Buccaneers in 1980, a number of Hunters were operated in lieu. By 15 December 1981, XF386 had been allocated the maintenance serial 8707M at Coltishall, Norfolk; subsequently moved to the Otterburn Ranges, Northumberland in 1986, it gradually expired over the ensuing decade or so.* Chris Salter collection

Above: *Hunter F.6 XF414 'P', No.63 Squadron, 20 September 1958. Although the Squadron's distinctive yellow and black checks are prominently displayed on the fuselage, those on the wingtip remain less so. A month after this photograph was taken, the Squadron had been disbanded and XF414 joined No.56 Squadron – both units being based at Waterbeach, Cambridgeshire, at that time. No.63 Squadron would soon re-emerge within the DFCS as a shadow squadron and, later still, would reappear as a component of No.229 OCU. XF414 was converted to FGA.9 standard in 1961 and issued to No.20 Squadron. It was lost following a power loss shortly after take-off in Malaya on 20 February 1967.* Newark Air Museum

Hunter F.6 XF417 'B', and F.6 XE530 'A', both from No.26 Squadron, 1959. XF417 was delivered in December 1955, but was then presumably stored prior to being allocated to No.14 Squadron in May 1958 at Ahlhorn, West Germany. It remained with that unit for a month before being transferred to No.26 Squadron which had reformed on 7 June 1958 with Hunters at Ahlhorn. (Sources conflict re this latter point, but No.26 Squadron did reform at Ahlhorn - not Gutersloh). Both units transferred to Gutersloh, West Germany during September 1958, where No.26 disbanded on 30 December 1960. XF417 had been stored by January 1961 and transferred to Jordan by October 1962. XE530 was first flown on 28 December 1955 and subsequently allocated to Rolls-Royce for engine trials. Thereafter, as with XF417, the aircraft served with No.14 Squadron from May 1958 prior to being allocated to No.26 Squadron one month later. It was converted to FGA.9 standard during 1961/62, after which, other than a period in storage, it served with Nos.208 and 43 Squadrons and was ultimately sold to Kuwait in 1969. The No.26 Squadron Motif displayed on the Hunter's nose, with bars, is a springboks head. Their motto translated reads 'A guard in the sky'.
John Merry via Tony Buttler

Above: *Hunter FR.10 XF426 '12', No.229 OCU, seen at Finningley 12 August 1968. Its white dorsal spine was used to identify an instructors aircraft when 'jumping' their students in mock combat. Built as an F.6 and delivered on 9 January 1956, this Hunter was placed in storage for a lengthy period prior to serving with No.208 Squadron for a short period. In 1960 it was modified to FR.10 standard and returned to service in early 1961. The following four years remain thin in detail, although it seems not to have served with any FR.10 equipped squadrons. It is known however to have served at Boscombe Down from April or May 1965 for approximately two years, following which, XF426 was allocated to No.229 OCU, its last British operator. Thereafter, it was presented* to Jordan and, later still, passed on to Oman where it was retired circa 1993. In 2003, the FR.10 was presented to the RAF Museum, Hendon as an exhibit. Chris Salter collection

Below: *An unidentified Hunter from No.54 Squadron, possibly XF446 that was known to have served with this unit and was coded 'B'. The Squadron Motif is a lion rampant which faced forward on both the port and starboard sides of the nose. The Squadron's motto translated is 'Boldness to endure anything'. The Squadron bars consist of Roundel Blue and yellow checks which have been repeated on the nose wheel door above the code letter; the wingtips appear to be plain white.* Tony Buttler collection

Above: *Hunter F.6 XF453 'V', DFCS, location not known, circa 1960/61. Delivered to Kemble on 8 March 1956, this aircraft served with Nos.247 and 54 Squadrons, followed by the AFDS, FCS and DFCS. The latter unit used the shadow designations No.122 Squadron until mid-1959 and No.63 Squadron afterwards. XF453 was coded 'V' by the DFCS whilst based at West Raynham and bears No.63 Squadron's Motif on its nose within miniature bars, (see XF414 for a comparison on page 37). The Motif consists of a forearm and hand grasping a battleaxe and their motto translated* read 'Follow us to find the enemy'. *The DFCS, with its parent body the CFE, moved to Binbrook, Lincolnshire in November 1962 and disbanded there in November 1965. Consequently most of the ex-DFCS aircraft and aircrew joined No.229 OCU where No.63 Squadron became the OCU's Weapon Instructor Flight, although there is no apparent record of XF453 ever having served with No.229 OCU. It is known however that the aircraft was bought by the manufacturers in July 1967 and sold to Chile a year later.*
Author's collection

Opposite bottom and above: *Hunter XF523 'N', No.54 Squadron, early 1960s. Built as an F.6 and delivered on 15 November 1956, it was operated only by No.54 Squadron, both prior to and following its modification to FGA.9 standard. In early 1960, both Nos.1 and 54 Squadrons had their roles recast to provide tactical air support and were incorporated into No.38 (Air Support) Group, Transport Command. Their primary weapon for ground attack duties – for which the FGA.9 had been epitomised, was the 3in rocket, 16 of which can be seen here, carried in two tiers. Later they were replaced by Matra-type rocket pods. This aircraft was* destroyed when it crashed on 24 June 1963 at Benina Airport in Libya. The pilot was killed. *Tony Buttler collection*

Below: *Hunter F.4 XF970, ETPS, Farnborough c1966. First flown in May 1956, this aircraft was operated by Nos.130, 234 and 26 Squadrons and No.229 OCU before joining the ETPS. In May 1967 XF970 went to No.1 SoTT as an instructional airframe becoming 7936M. Thereafter it was purchased by Hawker Siddeley Aviation (HSA) in 1971 and sold to Singapore in 1972.*
Chris Salter collection

Right: *Hunter F.4 XF994, No.66 Squadron, seen at Syerston, Nottinghamshire, September 1956. Delivered on 27 July 1956, this aircraft went first to No.66 Squadron in August 1956 prior to being transferred to the AFDS during the following November. Later it served with No.229 OCU before being converted for the FAA. As a T.8C, XF994 served initially with No.759 Squadron coded 655/BY and thereafter was used by several FAA squadrons as well as the Fleet Requirements & Air Direction Unit (FRADU) until placed in storage in 1995. Three years later it was moved by road to Boscombe Down were it served as an instructional airframe for apprentices. Today XF994 is owned by Hawker Hunter Aviation Ltd and re-entered the military register in early 2010. The Motif on the nose is most probably a coiled rattlesnake as featured in No.66 Squadrons Badge; their motto translated reads 'Beware, I have given warning'.* Newark Air Museum

Centre right: *Hunter FGA.9 XG130 'E', No.1 Squadron, circa 1962. Built as an F.6, first flown in August 1956, XG130 was operated in turn by Nos.66, 63 and 56 Squadrons. In 1959 it was returned to the manufacturer and later converted to an FGA.9. In 1962 it returned to service and was allocated in turn to Nos.1, 54, 208 and 45 Squadrons. It was abandoned in flight near Melton Mowbray, Leicestershire on 17 June 1974 as a result of pilot disorientation in cloud.* Chris Salter collection

Right: *Close-up of a No.1 Squadron's Hunter nose markings represented by a winged numeral 1. Their motto translated reads 'First in all things'.* Mike Harris collection via Simon Watson

Top: *Hunter F.6 XG161 'P', DFLS (?), Binbrook,
dated 7 October 1964. Assuming this date to be
correct, the DFLS had disbanded in 1958 becoming
the DFCS in its stead. However, there appears to be
no record of this aircraft having served with the
latter unit, which may possibly indicate an
omission in the record. Certainly XG161 was coded
'P' whilst with the DFLS; it also bears the 'shadow'
No.63 Squadron's Motif on its nose within
miniature bars. The 'yellow' Hunter is XG204 'B'
(see separate entry on page 45) which served both
the DFLS and DFCS in turn. Apparently the DFLS
had originally applied red paint to their A Flight
Hunters and yellow to B Flight; presumably this
practice was continued by the DFCS. XG161 went
on to serve with No.229 OCU and, whilst with this
unit, crashed into the sea off Cornwall on 14
February 1974 during formation flying practice;*

*the pilot was killed. The tanker is a Leyland Hippo
10 ton pressure-aircraft-refuelling vehicle.*
Newark Air Museum

Above: *Hunter F.6 XG164 'H', No.74 Squadron.
Delivered on 9 November 1956, this aircraft served
with Nos. 111, 74 and 1 Squadrons, Station Flight
West Raynham, No.229 OCU (twice) No.4 FTS
and the TWU. It subsequently became a ground
instruction airframe receiving the maintenance
serial 8681M and today survives in preservation.
Seen in its heyday, XG164 bears the No.74
Squadron tiger's face Motif and bars upon its nose.
Their appropriate motto translated reads 'I fear no
man'. The code 'H' is painted black on the nose
wheel door and (just visible) in yellow on the tail.*
Tony Buttler collection

Top: *Hunter F.6 XG172 'B', No.19 Squadron. Delivered in September 1956, this aircraft served first with No.19 Squadron, followed by No.263 Squadron which operated the Hunter F.6 but was disbanded on 1 July 1958. Presumably therefore, this photograph was taken circa 1957. Thereafter XG172 was operated by No.229 OCU and the TWU at Brawdy. According to some sources it was modified to F.6A standard (or if preferred interim FGA.9), but seems not to have become an FGA.9 per se ! Subsequently the aircraft became a ground instructional airframe at Scampton by September 1984 and received the maintenance serial 8832M; it later entered into preservation representing FR.10 'XG168'. In this image XG172 displays No.19 Squadron's blue and white checks on either side of both the fuselage roundel and the Squadron Badge on the nose; the latter features a dolphin with its* head downwards. The wingtips are white and incorporate a thin blue lightning flash. *Author's collection*

Above: *Hunter F.6 XG196 '31', No.229 OCU / No.234 (shadow) Squadron. (See XE591 re this unit). Delivered in October 1956, XG196 served with No.19 Squadron, No.229 OCU, the TWU and later No.1 TWU. This latter unit was created when the TWU was divided into two on 31 July 1978; No.1 remained at Brawdy with Hunters and, increasingly, the BAe Hawk T.1, whilst No.2 TWU formed at Lossiemouth, Morayshire with an establishment of 30 Hunters transferred from Brawdy. XG196 later went to the RAF Staff College at Bracknell, Berkshire in December 1981 for display, then finally to Keogh Barracks, Mytchett, Hampshire.* Tony Buttler collection

Left and centre left and subject of 4-view artwork: *Hunter F.6 XG204 'B', DFCS/ No.63 (shadow) Squadron, on display at Finningley, 14 September 1963, with an array of weaponry. (Refer also to XG161 on page 43). Delivered on 25 October 1956, XG204 was operated by the DFLS coded 'B', DFCS and, following the latter's disbandment joined No.4 FTS (coded '70') by 1968. On 15 August 1969 the aircraft was destroyed when it crashed into the ground apparently out of control; no firm reason was established.*
Both Newark Air Museum

Bottom: *Hunter FR.10 XJ633 'K', No.4 Squadron, September 1966. Built as an F.6 and delivered in February 1957, this aircraft served with Nos.93, 65 and 66 Squadrons before being converted to an FR.10. XJ633 went on to serve with Nos.4 and 2 Squadrons and, RAF service complete, was repurchased in 1971, and later sold to Singapore. The FR.10's raison d'être was photo-reconnaissance, and for this the camera-nose housed three Vinten F.95 cameras which were backed-up by a voice recorder for the pilot to record any comments he made as a result of visual observations. The FR.10 retained their four cannon, both for ground-attack and self-defence purposes. No.4 Squadron's colours were striking, and the bars either side of the fuselage roundels were repeated on the nose which encompassed the Squadron Motif represented by a flash of lightning dividing a 'sun in splendour'. This is explained (in reference to the Squadron Badge), as the sun being divided into two sections; red and black, indicating round the clock operations, whilst the flash of lightning is indicative of speed. Their motto translated reads 'To see into the future'.*
Author's collection

Top: *Hunter T.7 XL568 'X', No.74 Squadron, Coltishall, 14 August 1960. Delivered in October 1958, this aircraft was first operated by No.74 Squadron who received it in late December 1958. It was entered into the Daily Mail London to Paris Air Race on 29 July 1959 and recorded the fastest time. In June 1960 the Squadron commenced its conversion to the Lightning F.1 but retained Hunter T.7s, XL568 and XL620 'Z'. XL568 remained with the Squadron until July 1966, during which time it was modified to T.7A standard. Thereafter the aircraft enjoyed a long and varied career during which it was operated by several units, the penultimate being No.237 (Buccaneer) OCU which disbanded on 1 October 1991. The OCU's duties were assumed by No.208 Squadron which used XL568 until its last ever flight in November 1993 when it was delivered to Cranwell for ground instructional duties as 9224M. In 2002 the Hunter was delivered to the RAF Museum, Cosford, Shropshire for preservation.*
Newark Air Museum

Above: *Hunter T.7 XL568 'X', No.74 Squadron, Coltishall, 13 August 1963. Offered for comparison, this photograph was taken almost exactly three years after the previous one, by which time Day-Glo orange had been liberally applied. At this stage XL568 was still a T.7, its modification to T.7A standard was undertaken during 1964/65. Gloster Meteor T.7 WA671, seen in the background, was also allocated to No.74 Squadron and was most probably used as a target-tug by this date; it was struck off charge in May 1964. A photograph of WA671 appears in 'British Military Aviation - The 1960s In Colour' by this author.*
Newark Air Museum

Above: *Hunter T.7 XL575 '80' No.229 OCU / No.234 (shadow) Squadron at Wyton, Huntingdonshire, 14 September 1963. Delivered in July 1958, this aircraft served with No.229 OCU (twice), the Fighter Command Instrument Rating Squadron (FCIRS) and No.4 FTS. While serving with the latter unit, XL575 crashed into high ground in poor visibility on 8 November 1971 in Dyfed, Wales. Both crew members were killed.* Newark Air Museum

Below: *Hunter T.7 XL586 'RS-90', No.229 OCU, c1959. First flown in June 1958 and delivered in August 1958, XL586 was operated by No.229 OCU, the TWU, No.1 TWU and No.2 TWU prior to being allocated to the Ministry of Defence (Procurement Executive) in April 1983. This aircraft later entered into preservation and today resides at the Riverside MOT Centre, Melksham, Wiltshire. The code 'RS' on XL586's fuselage band denoted No.229 OCU, as did the code 'ES' which was also used; a practice which continued until about 1960.* Tony Buttler collection

Above: *Unidentified (but possibly XG129) Hunter F.6 'F', No.111 Squadron. This Squadron received F.6s in late 1956 and, knowing they would form the RAF's aerobatic team for 1957, adopted an overall gloss black colour scheme for their aircraft. The team also adopted the name 'Black Arrows' and became perhaps the best known Hunter unit of all time. Although of poor quality, this image does convey something of the striking effectiveness of the all black colour scheme, broken only by national markings, tiny Squadron Badge and bars on the nose and an unobtrusive red code letter on the nose wheel door.* Author's collection

Below: *Three Hunter FGA.9s, No.45 Squadron. Late in the Hunter's life the type was allocated to No.45 Squadron which reformed in August 1972; the first time that the unit operated Hunters. A year later No.58 Squadron was similarly equipped, their combined purpose was to provide a pool of experienced ground-attack pilots. In June 1976 both units disbanded and their function was taken over by the TWU. No.45 Squadron's Emblem appears on the nose of each Hunter and displays a blue camel with red wings on a white disc flanked by bars. The significance of the camel relates to the Squadron's use of the Sopwith Camel during WWI and to the 21 years which the unit spent in the Middle East. Their motto translated reads 'Through difficulties I arise'.* Tony Buttler collection

A detailed image of No.65 Squadron's markings applied to the nose of unidentified Hunter F.6 'M'. This unit was equipped with Hunters from December 1956 until March 1961, the F.6 and two T.7s being the only variants received; obviously therefore, this photograph dates from that period. Their Motif consists of a lion in front of 15 gold swords, their hilts to the ground; representing a particular combat in which 15 enemy aircraft were destroyed. Their motto translated reads 'By force of arms'. Author's collection

Unidentified Hunter T.7 'Q', No.92 Squadron. Following the re-equipping of No.111 Squadron with Lightnings from April 1961, No.92 Squadron became the RAF's official aerobatic team for the 1961/62 seasons. They elected to paint their Hunters in gloss blue adorned by a slender white line along the length of the fuselage with white wingtips. This team became the 'Blue Diamonds'. In April 1963, they too received Lightnings although at least one Hunter T.7 was retained as a 'hack'. Chris Salter collection

A detailed image of No.92 Squadron's markings applied to the nose of an unidentified Hunter T.7. The cobra and maple leaf illustrated here is a variation of the Motif contained within the Squadron's Badge whose motto translated reads 'Either fight or die'. Author's collection

RAF Khormaksar, Aden.
The Hunters of Nos.8, 43, 208
Squadrons and No.1417 Flight.

The Aden Protectorate was a British colony and remained so until 30 November 1967. Britain's presence in Aden was backed by a continual and considerable military force whose role was, in tactical terms, to defend Aden and the Protectorates from external attack and to maintain law and order within the territory. From the RAF's perspective, the Hunter FGA.9 was an obvious type of aircraft with which to conduct ground-attack sorties in support of military operations in the region. As tensions in the area continued to rise however, a state of emergency was declared covering the Aden Protectorate in December 1963. Consequently, it became necessary to increase Britain's military presence in order to counter the increasing number of terrorist attacks and acts of lawlessness. This continued until Britain's withdrawal from Aden was promulgated in 1966, when the newly elected Labour government in the UK announced that all forces would be

withdrawn by 1968; RAF Khormaksar was closed on the 29 November 1967.

Throughout the period 1960 to 1967, three Hunter FGA.9 Squadrons were resident at Khormaksar for varying lengths of time. These were: No.8 Squadron (1953-1967; Hunter FGA.9s replaced DH Venoms in 1960), No.43 Squadron (March 1963 - November 1967), No.208 Squadron (December 1961- June 1964). Four Hunter FR.10s were released from No.8 Squadron in March 1963 to form No.1417 (Fighter Reconnaissance) Flight at Khormaksar which, in addition, also incorporated the Station Flight's four T.7s. The Flight was absorbed into No.8 Squadron on 8 September 1967. The combined resident units are variously referred to as the Khormaksar Hunter Wing, the Khormaksar Tactical Wing or the Aden Strike Wing. The author has been unable to confirm if any of the three were officially authorised titles and there may have been more; doubtless any or all would have become usefully descriptive phrases in the 1960s.

The following selection of photographs were (mostly) taken at Khormaksar and are all from the Mike Harris collection.

Hunter FR.10 XE614, 'RJ', No.1417 Flight. A feature of the Flight's aircraft was the codes they carried - they were the individual pilot's initials. This aircraft carries a cautionary chalked inscription below the cockpit 'NO HYDRAULICS'. XE614 went to Singapore in 1973.

In an apparent contradiction to this section's Aden theme, these images are those of two No.208 Squadron FGA.9s, XE552 'D' and XE643 'K', which came to grief at Mombasa, Kenya on 9 December 1961. At this time the Squadron was based in Aden and had been for a little under one month, so presumably they were either on a temporary detachment or were staging through. It is known that XE643 lost power during take-off at Mombasa and the take-off was abandoned. The braking parachute was deployed and the main undercarriage raised, but these measures could not prevent the aircraft from overshooting. It was written-off following this accident. As for XE552, there would appear to be no record of its involvement in an accident at this time. The photograph speaks for itself though; the starboard undercarriage has either collapsed or sunk into the grass and the braking parachute deployed. XE552 survived and was later operated by Nos.1 and 2 TWU; it crashed into the sea north of Lossiemouth on 23 February 1981 killing the pilot.

Top: Hunter T.7 XF321 'TZ', with hybrid Nos.8/43 Squadron markings on the fuselage and No.1417 Flight's 'arrowhead' on its nose. This aircraft also appears in the previous Hunter section.

Above: Hunter FGA.9 XF376 'Q' with No.8 Squadron's and No.208 Squadron's colours borne on the fuselage and nose respectively, as compared with XE609 'E' beyond which bears only the latter unit's colours. XF376 survived to return to the UK and was used by No.229 OCU, and all three TWUs. It was sold to Chile in May 1982. XE609 overshot when it caught fire during its landing approach to Khormaksar on 5 April 1966 and was not repaired.

Left: For a time No.208 Squadron's colours were applied to their FGA.9s in this form. The sphinx Motif features in No.208 Squadron's Badge whose motto reads simply 'Vigilant', a term inspired by both the sphinx and the Squadron's long association with Egypt. No.8 Squadron's Badge appears beneath the pilot's name and shows an Arabian dagger sheathed, it being indicative of the unit's long association with Arabia. Their motto translated reads 'Everywhere unbounded'.

Above: *Hunter FGA.9 XG169 'K', No.43 Squadron. Following its service at Khormaksar with each of its resident squadrons, XG169 returned to the UK but was lost on 5 June 1963 over Devon following an engine failure. The pilot ejected safely.*

Left: *Camera port and nose detail of Hunter FR.10 'DB', No.1417 Flight. The transport in the left background is a Hawker Siddeley Andover C.1.*

Left: *No.1417 (Fighter Reconnaissance) Flight's colours incorporating the Royal Air Force Station Khormaksar Badge.*

Opposite top: *Hunter FGA.9 XJ692 'T', with hybrid Nos.8/43 Squadron markings. XJ692 was delivered to India in 1969.*

Opposite centre: *Hunter FGA.9 XK140 'D', of No.208 Squadron. Showing evidence of having recently fired its guns, XK140 displays the Squadron colours on bars, outlined in black, each side of the fuselage roundel as opposed to the arrowhead design previously used. According to one source, it is possible that this image was taken in April or May 1967 during this Hunter's third term with this unit for which it received the code 'D'; previously it had been coded 'E', then 'H'. Subsequently XK140 returned to the UK and was operated by No.45 Squadron then No.2 TWU; it was abandoned in flight over the sea on 3 July 1979.*

Opposite bottom: *Hunter T.7 XL566 'TW' No.1417 Flight with hybrid Nos.8/43 Squadron markings. This aircraft later served with No.208 Squadron. It ultimately returned to the UK, though sources conflict as to its subsequent service. It is believed however that it*

was with the Laarbruch Station Flight in 1980/81 and then passed to the RN from November 1981. It was returned to RAF charge in 1986 becoming 8891M at Bruggen, West Germany, and scrapped there in 1995.

Top: *Hunter T.7 XL566 once more, now coded 'Y' of No.208 Squadron, with (presumably) a replacement tail cone.*

Above: *Hunter T.7 XL612 'T', No.8 Squadron, October 1967. On its return to the UK, XL612 went ultimately to the ETPS with which it made its last flight in 2001 and was subsequently sold into preservation.*

Top: *Unidentified Hunter FGA.9 'U' No.54 Squadron. As stated earlier, (see XF523 on pages 40/41) although based principally in the UK, Nos.1 and 54 Squadrons had had their roles recast in 1960 to provide a tactical air support element within No.38 (Air Support) Group, Transport Command, and were temporarily despatched to Aden as required.*

Above: *Unidentified Hunter FGA.9s on Nos.1, 54 and 208 Squadrons*

Opposite top: *Hunter T.8C WT702, '874/VL', FRADU early 1982. Built as an F.4 and retained by the MoS for radio trials, WT702 was converted to a T.8 and then delivered to the FAA in June 1959, thereafter serving with a host of units. It had been upgraded to T.8C standard by May 1966. WT702's final user was the FRADU at*

Yeovilton with which it served many times from 1972 onwards interspersed with periods at MUs, and received several different codes over the ensuing years. Its final code was '874/VL' which it received in August 1979. WT702 was destroyed when it flew into the sea near the Isle of Wight in December 1982 whilst conducting exercises with HMS Exeter. *Tony O'Toole collection*

Opposite bottom: *Hunter T.8, '871/VL', FRADU. The previous image of WT702 fails to fully communicate the colour scheme adopted by FAA T.8s, which replaced the earlier overall silver with yellow training bands scheme. Although this is a familiar image, it perfectly conveys the striking nature of the later scheme. This aircraft is not WT702 but colourwise the two are virtually identical, under-wing tanks excepted. Tony O'Toole collection*

Fleet Air Arm Hunters

The Royal Navy's Fleet Air Arm made considerable use of the Hunter as a second-line aircraft, adopting a number of marks and colour schemes in the process. The following short photo-selection will hopefully suffice to provide a flavour of a bygone era.

Right: *Hunter T.8 WT722, '742/VL', 5 September 1970, Air Direction Training Unit, Yeovilton. Although 'BY' is seen on the fin, it refers to a previous user at Brawdy and was removed and replaced by 'VL'. A panel beneath the cockpit has been over-painted with '742'. Built as an F.4 and delivered in May 1955 to No.54 Squadron, it was later converted to a T.8 and delivered to the FAA in June 1959; sources conflict as to whether or not it was further upgraded. It was sold into preservation in August 1995.* Tony O'Toole collection

Opposite centre: *Hunter PR.11 WT723, '692/LM' No.764 Squadron, Lossiemouth, Moray, 1970. The chequered markings on the nose are superimposed with the Squadron Motif a 'Balance Gold', i.e. scales, just forward of which and slightly below is a camera port. The aircraft's white spine was an embellishment applied to some GA/PR.11s, but not all. Originally built as an F.4 and first flown on 16 February 1954, this aircraft operated with Nos.54 and 14 Squadrons before passing to No.229 OCU. Following service with the RAF, WT723 was converted to a GA.11 for the FAA and allocated to No.764 Squadron at Lossiemouth on 17 September 1962, coded '696/LM'; the Squadron's principal role was Air Warfare Instructor training. In July 1967, the aircraft underwent modernisation and a change of code to '692/LM' and it is possible that it was modified to become a PR.11 at this time too. Following No.764 Squadron's disbandment on 27 July 1972, WT723 was (ultimately) transferred to the FRADU at Yeovilton, Somerset. It remained with FRADU until withdrawn from use in 1995 and subsequently sold into preservation.* Newark Air Museum

Opposite bottom: *Hunter GA.11 WT804, '831/VL' FRADU, Yeovilton, July 1977. Following conversion, this aircraft entered FAA service with No.738 Squadron at Lossiemouth in September 1962. Later, as seen here, WT804 served with FRADU and remained with them until placed in storage in March 1982, after which it was used for ground handling and appears not to have flown again, although it was maintained for taxying purposes until 1994. Today it resides at Moreton-in-Marsh airfield, Gloucestershire, displayed in a nose-in-the-turf attitude!* Tony O'Toole collection

Top and above: *These two images exemplify the principal differences between the Harley light-equipped GA.11 '864/VL' and the camera-nose equipped PR.11 '866/VL'. Although undated, the application of the colour scheme shown dates from the early 1980s and included a change from Type D national markings to Type B as seen on XF310 '869/VL'.* Both Tony O'Toole collection

Top: *Hunter T.8 WW664, seen at Farnborough, September 1958. This aircraft was the prototype Hunter T.8 and first flew as such on 3 March 1958. By May 1958, it was at Boscombe Down being tested for the RN in relation to the type's suitability as well as weapons, UHF radio and airfield arrester hook trials. Later, WW664 became the prototype T.8B and was heavily involved with early TACAN trials at Boscombe Down. From mid-1961 it commenced service with a number of FAA squadrons until, on 31 October 1969, WW664 suffered an engine fire on take-off, forcing the pilot to eject with fatal consequences. The aircraft was written-off.* Tony Buttler collection

Above: *Hunter T.7 XF310, '869/VL', mid-1992. Built as an F.4, this aircraft was used during 1956 in trials with the Fairey Fireflash beam-riding air-to-air missile, of which it could carry two. Following the trials, it was converted to a T.7 and served with the RAF from mid-1959 until mid-1969; thereafter it was loaned to the RN and later returned to the RAF. This set a trend over the following years as XF310 alternated between one service or the other, was loaned to the A&AEE, or placed in long-term storage. XF310 made its last flight in March 1993 and became a ground instructional airframe. It was finally withdrawn from use in early 1997 and later sold into preservation. In this image XF310 was in use by FRADU, being one of nine T.7s transferred for naval duties, albeit that some were retained in long-term storage or used as ground instructional airframes.* Tony O'Toole collection

Top: *Hunter T.8M XL580, '717/VL', Yeovilton. One of ten T.8s built as such and operated by a number of units before being converted to a T.8C in 1965/66 and further modified to a T.8M from 1980. XL580 was one of three T.8M conversions intended for Blue Fox radar training, as fitted to the Sea Harrier FRS.1. On 7 August 1981, XL580 joined No.899 Squadron at Yeovilton which had reformed in 1980 equipped with Sea Harriers. Initially XL580 was coded '717/VL', then '719/VL' and '723' by early 1992; it made its last flight in 1993 and in 1994 went to the FAA Museum. This image shows XL580 in No.899 Squadron's markings, the Motif on the tail is a variation of the winged gauntlet which appears on the Squadron Badge and whose motto is 'Strike and defend'. A Sidewinder air-to-air missile acquisition round is fitted on the port pylon. An arrestor hook, for land use only, is fitted to the fuselage.*

Above: *Full Circle. Hunter ZZ191, seen at Yeovilton with a second Hunter and four F-16s beyond. The Hunters are the property of 'Hawker Hunter Aviation Ltd' (HHA), ZZ191, ZZ192 and ZZ194 being ex-Swiss Mk.58s. They, along with XF994 and XF995 have been entered, (or re-entered in the case of the latter two) onto the UK military register for the purposes of Contractualised Fast Jet Air Support. Further Mk.58 Hunters are due to join them. Despite their vintage, during the last four years HHA's Hunters have exhibited a 99% sortie success rate and are in the process of being upgraded with very modern systems to further enhance their training value to the UK's armed forces. These Hunters possess a performance in excess of that found in many more modern jets and have, remarkably, very few 'hours on the clock'. There definitely remains a lot of life in their old airframes. Both Tony O'Toole collection*

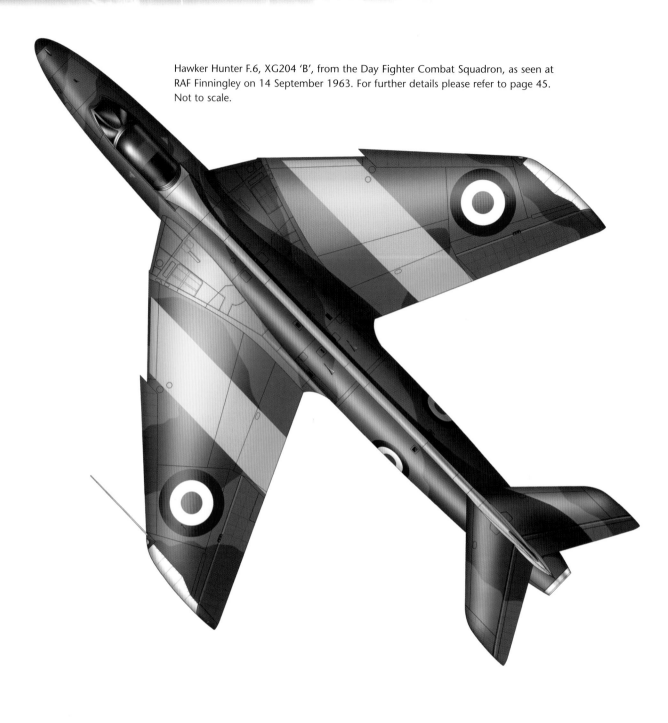

Hawker Hunter F.6, XG204 'B', from the Day Fighter Combat Squadron, as seen at RAF Finningley on 14 September 1963. For further details please refer to page 45. Not to scale.

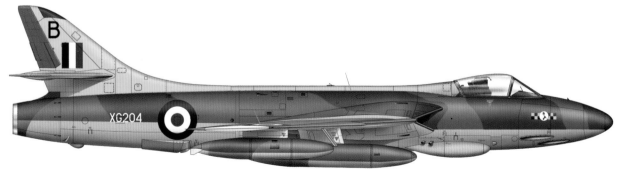

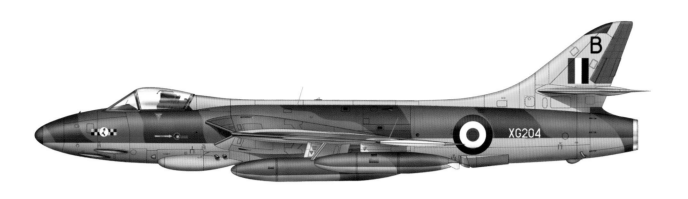

3 De Havilland Vampire T.11

The Vampire T.11 was based on de Havilland's earlier single-seat Vampire FB.5 fighter-bomber and utilised the latter's wings and tail booms. Additionally, it incorporated experience gained with the Vampire NF.10 night-fighter which featured a two-seat, (virtually) side-by-side seating arrangement for the crew members, an arrangement deemed suitable for the training role with appropriate modification. The T.11 was fitted with dual controls, dual instrumentation and, in order that the aircraft might cover as many training roles as possible, retained the four 20mm cannon of its predecessors, (sometimes just two) plus the ability to carry bombs and rockets when required, thus enhancing its utility in an operational role if necessary.

The first example of its type was a manufacturer's private venture designed to meet with the RAF's advanced training requirements whilst retaining as much in common with other Vampire variants as possible. Registered as G-5-7, it was first flown on 15 November 1950, then later delivered to the RAF for trials receiving the serial WW456, (which is excluded from most serial listings). The trials were successfully completed by late April 1951 and the aircraft was ultimately adopted by the RAF and designated Vampire T.11. Production orders followed and the first production T.11, WZ414, made its maiden flight in January 1952, with service deliveries commencing in September 1952 to No.202 AFS at RAF Valley. From the 144th production T.11 a number of modifications were incorporated into the design, the most important being: the fitting of dorsal fairings extending forward from the fin along the tail booms, a moulded single-piece canopy and, the fitting of ejector seats. Several earlier T.11s received these modifications retrospectively.

Ultimately, as more became available, the Vampire T.11 was issued to scores of RAF units including training schools, conversion units, communication flights, station flights, anti-aircraft co-operation units and a miscellany of other bodies. The T.11 was also allocated to a large number of operational RAF squadrons as hacks, including some to the Royal Auxiliary Air Force until that organisation's demise in March 1957, although by late 1959 the T.11 had largely, although not entirely disappeared from most of the regular squadrons too. By the start of the 1960s therefore, the period with which this volume is principally concerned, the T.11 was largely involved, in ever diminishing quantities, with training and subsidiary duties until the mid-1960s.

By 1965, relatively few Vampire T.11s remained with the RAF, although a half dozen or so resided with No.1 FTS at Linton-on-Ouse, principally for the training of overseas students. Their surviving T.11s, plus some held in store, were transferred to join those of No.7 FTS at Church Fenton in 1966, until transferred in turn to No.3 FTS at Leeming (all three bases being located in Yorkshire) on 30 November 1966, following the disbandment of No.7 FTS. The T.11's last FTS sortie was conducted on November 29 1967. Elsewhere, other than ground-instructional, stored or display airframes, T.11s continued to fly with the Central Air Traffic Control School (CATCS) at Shawbury, Shropshire, until late 1970 and with

No.3/4 Civilian Anti-Aircraft Co-operation Unit (CAACU) at Exeter, which continued in existence until 31 December 1971.

Sea Vampire T.22

In addition to the RAF, the Royal Navy also identified a need for the Vampire trainer and so two pre-production T.11 airframes, WW458 & WW461 were procured for RN evaluation. These were retained and probably redesignated Vampire T.22 as opposed to *Sea Vampire*, whereas the production aircraft were designated Sea Vampire T.22. The latter differed from the T.11 in as much that certain minor modifications were incorporated for naval use, excluding arrestor hooks, as they were not intended for use aboard aircraft carriers. Ejector seats were fitted retrospectively from 1956. The first production order for 53 T.22s was placed on 8 February 1952 and the first of their number, XA100, flew in May 1953, although it was the fourth example, XA103, which first entered FAA service in October 1953. A second production batch of 20 T.22s was ordered in June 1954.

In service, unsurprisingly, the T.22 was used for much the same purposes as was the T.11 within the RAF: pilot training, instrument rating, trials, communications, station flights etc.

Vampire T.11 WZ571 '52', Syerston, Nottinghamshire, September 1965. Delivered in May 1953, this aircraft had previously been operated by No.229 OCU, Odiham's Station Flight, Linton-on-Ouse Station Flight, CFS and Nos.1 and 5 FTS. WZ571's flying days were over by the time this image was taken and had been struck off charge four months earlier and allocated for fire practice at Syerston, where it eventually expired. Newark Air Museum

T.22s served with eight or more operational squadrons (particularly those equipped with Sea Venoms), and with at least two Royal Navy Volunteer Reserve squadrons.

The T.22's withdrawal from service was underway by 1965 and the last (flying) example, XA129, was withdrawn in July 1970, its final duties being with the Air Direction Training Unit run by civilian operated Airwork Limited at Yeovilton. Two other long-term survivors were XG769 and XG743: the former finished its naval service with the Lossiemouth Station Flight in March 1970, following which it went into storage until sold to Chile in 1972, whilst the latter finished its flying days with Brawdy's Station Flight. Sources conflict somewhat with regard to XG743's final flights, however its logbook reveals that on 2 November 1970 it was ferried to No.5 MU at Kemble for storage. It was transferred by road to the Imperial War Museum on 13 March 1972, which may indicate therefore that XG743 (and possibly other examples) was flying until November 1970, several months after XA129's last flight !

Opposite top: *Vampire T.11 WZ590 '19', No.8 FTS, being refuelled at Swinderby during September 1962, with a Meteor and at least one other Vampire visible in the distance. Number 8 FTS had been reformed out of No.203 Advanced Flying School (AFS) at Driffield, Yorkshire, in June 1954 equipped with Meteors initially, with Vampires, Hunting Percival Provosts, Varsity T.1s and Handley Page Marathon T.1s being added later. In August 1955 the unit moved to Swinderby and remained there until disbanded in March 1964. WZ590 was delivered on 12 December 1953 and initially served with No.228 OCU, followed by No.5 FTS and finally No.8 FTS. It was sold in 1968 and, after a period of storage, was preserved.* Author's collection

Opposite bottom and above: *Two views of Sea Vampire T.22 XA129, seen at Hatfield on 13 July 1968. This T.22 was amongst the last flying examples of its type (but see T.22 introduction) and, when these images were obtained, was being operated by Airwork Ltd, who had received it in March 1968. XA129 had spent the previous 17 months in storage at Kemble, preceded by, amongst others, service with Nos.738 and 736 Squadrons and the Flag Officer Flying Training Flight. Although it is not apparent in these images in which even the serial is hard to discern, this aircraft was allocated the code '747/VL', which presumably had yet to be applied. XA129 was struck off charge on 7 July 1970 and subsequently entered into preservation.* Both Newark Air Museum

Vampire T.11 serial allocations:

Prototype (ex-G-5-7): WW456.

Pre-production Vampire T.11s, (later Vampire T.22s): WW458 & WW461.

Production aircraft: WZ414-WZ430, WZ446-478, WZ493-521, WZ544-WZ593, WZ607-WZ620. (143 x T.11 in WZ range. All entered British service. Approximately 26 written-off as a result of accidents/incidents.)

XD375-XD405, XD424-XD463, XD506-XD554, XD588-XD627. (160 x T.11 in XD range. All entered British service. Approximately 28 written-off as a result of accidents/incidents.)

XE816-XE833, XE848-XE897, XE919-XE961, XE975-XE998. (135 x T.11 in XE range. 123 entered British service. Approximately 23 written-off as a result of accidents / incidents. 12 aircraft: XE816-XE819, XE823-XE826 & XE938-XE941 were diverted to the Southern Rhodesian Air Force, later Royal Rhodesian Air Force [RRAF].)

XH264-XH278, XH292-XH330, XH357-XH368. (66 x T.11 in XH range. 57 entered British service. Approximately 9 written-off as a result of accidents/incidents and includes XH304. It and Meteor WA669 both from the CFS, together formed the 'Vintage Pair'; but they collided and crashed on 25 May 1986. XH265, XH266, XH271, XH317 and XH366 were diverted to the Royal New Zealand Air Force. XH268-XH270 and XH275 went to the RRAF.)

XJ771-XJ776 (6 x T.11 from a frustrated Norwegian order and taken into British service during 1955.)

XK582-XK590, XK623-XK637. (24 x T.11 in XK range. All entered British service. 4 written-off as a result of accidents/incidents.)

T.11 Production Total (excluding Prototype and Pre-production aircraft) = 534 of which approximately 90 were written-off as a result of accidents/incidents.

Sea Vampire T.22 serial allocations:

XA100-XA131, XA152-XA172. (53 x T.22 in XA range. All entered RN service.)

XG742-XG748, XG765-XG777. (20 x T.22 in XG range. All entered RN service.)

T.22 Production Total = 73 of which approximately 14 were written-off as a result of accidents/incidents.

Left: *Unidentified Vampire T.11 from the XD serial range in mid-1962.*

Below left: *Vampire T.11 XE857 '49', No.4 FTS, at Hucknall, Nottinghamshire, 3 June 1962. Delivered in February 1954, XE857 served in turn with Nos.4, 7, 5, 4, 1, 7 and 3 FTS before joining the CATCS at Shawbury, following which it was stored then sold to Chile in November 1972. By the time that this photograph was taken, '49' was operating with No.4 FTS; their Badge, seen near the cockpit consists of a palm tree in front of a pyramid. By August 1962, No.4 FTS had completely replaced their Vampires with Folland Gnats and XE857 was transferred to No.1 FTS and then to No.7 FTS at Church Fenton, which was equipped principally with Jet Provosts and more properly known as No.7 (Basic) Flying Training School. However, as described in the introduction, a few Vampire T.11s were retained, of which XE857 was one; by then numbered '54'. Number 7 FTS was disbanded on 30 November 1966 and its remaining Vampires moved to No.3 FTS at Leeming where XE857 received the code number '64'. Both Newark Air Museum*

Opposite top: *Sea Vampire T.22 XA153, Brawdy dump, 20 July 1963. Delivered in May 1954 this Sea Vampire served with several units, mostly station flights, although it did serve with No.727 Squadron at Brawdy coded '556/BY'. However, in February 1963 it was declared as surplus and awaiting disposal and had clearly seen better days when this photograph was taken, although, other than the cockpit canopy, externally at least it still seemed to be in a reasonable condition. It lingered on the dump until June 1965 when it was sold for scrap.* Author's collection

Opposite centre: *Vampire T.11 XD443 '44', RAF College Cranwell (RAFC), Lincolnshire. Delivered on 10 February 1954, this T.11 was first issued to No.7 FTS prior to being allocated to the RAFC who applied their distinctive pale blue bands to the tail booms. Thereafter, XD443 served with the CFS then No.8 FTS; it was sold for scrap at No.27 MU, Shawbury in March 1965. Just to add confusion to the apparent certainty that this was an RAFC aircraft when photographed, the badge below the*

cockpit - although indistinct, colour wise and proportionally looks remarkably similar to No.8 FTS's Badge, which consisted of a central red disc on a white ground impaled by crossed keys ! Author's collection

Opposite bottom: *Vampire T.11 XD542 'H'. Delivered in July 1954, XD542 served with the Central Gunnery School (CGS) and then with the Fighter Weapons School (FWS). The CGS disbanded on 31 December 1954, but morphed into the FWS the following day, its purpose being to train pilots in the use of guns, bombs and rockets. Based initially at Leconfield, Yorkshire, the FWS moved to Driffield in October 1957, then merged with the CFE in March 1958. Although this image is undated, XD542 had become a ground instructional airframe by June 1959 with the maintenance serial 7604M, so it is likely that this image pre-dates 1959. 7604M survived both ground instructional and gate guard duties long enough to enter into preservation at Montrose, Angus in 1997.* Author's collection

Top and above: *Vampire T.11 XE920 'D'. Delivered in February 1955 this aircraft was first operated by the Allied Air Forces Central Europe Communications Flight at Melun-Villaroche, France. Thereafter it served with Nos.5 and 8 FTS and finally with the CATCS at Shawbury, with which unit XE920 is seen here. The two images were apparently taken at Cranwell, borne out perhaps by the presence of pale blue bands on the fuselages of the Jet Provosts and Vickers Varsity in the background. The date is cautiously given as May 1970 – this might just be possible as the CATCS continued to use T.11s until late 1970, being virtually the last RAF unit, as opposed to civilian operated units, to fly Vampires. The T.11 in the background coded 'T' might be XE919; if so, it too was a long-lived CATCS aircraft which was sold in February 1971. XE920 subsequently became a ground instructional airframe at Shawbury as 8196M and was later preserved.* Both Newark Air Museum

Opposite: *Three images taken at Swinderby of No.8 FTS Vampire T.11s; the first in 1962 and the second and third in March 1964. The latter image was taken just a few days prior to No.8 FTS' disbandment on 19 March 1964, by which time the style of Day-Glo applications had been altered by comparison with the earlier image. The aircraft fleet numbers had also been high-lighted. XE927 '14' was struck off charge a month later, whilst the flying example, XK627 '38', presumably went into storage until sold in 1968. Its cockpit section has been preserved.*
All Newark Air Museum

Above: Vampire T.11 XH367, RAFC. Seen at Leconfield. Delivered in May 1956 XH367 spent its entire operational life with the RAFC at Cranwell before being sold for scrap at Shawbury in March 1964. Vampires were sometimes referred to in the RAF as the 'Kiddy Car', which is a less surprising nickname when compared in size to the Gloster Javelins beyond. The Javelins are FAW.4s of No.72 Squadron which operated this type at Leconfield from June 1959 until June 1961 when the unit disbanded, thus helping to narrow down the date of the photograph somewhat. Author's collection

Below: Vampire T.11 XK624 '32', CFS seen at Hatfield in mid-1969. Delivered in 1956, XK624 was operated by a large number of units before arriving with the CFS (its second time) which, when this photograph was taken, was based at Little Rissington, Gloucestershire, having reformed there in 1946. The distinctive CFS Motif is very evident on the Vampire's nose; far more discreet is the aircraft's individual code number seen below the port rudder. XK624 remained at Little Rissington until at least September 1971. It was sold three months later and subsequently entered into preservation. Chris Salter collection

Right: A vintage pair. XK624 and Meteor T.7 WA669 '27'. Possibly photographed at Little Rissington in 1971, this information is tentative at best however as it is based solely on the handwritten characters 'L-R71' found on the frame of the slide. WA669 was fated to collide with Vampire T.11 XH304, when, as the 'Vintage Pair', they came together and crashed during an air display at Mildenhall, Suffolk, on 25 May 1986.
Author's collection

Three images of Vampire T.11s operated by No.3/4 CAACU, seen at Exeter Airport during the mid-1960s. In July 1954, two separate CAACU's, No.3 at Exeter and No.4 at Llandow, Glamorgan, were combined to form No.3/4 CAACU based at Exeter and equipped with several ex-World War II types – the most famous arguably being the DH Mosquito. Jet aircraft were later introduced to offer more realistic target speeds, of which the Vampire T.11 was one. The three T.11s shown here are all fitted with under-wing fuel tanks for extended range with XK632 '67' and XH328 '66' seen near the control tower, whilst XH304 '71' was at a dispersal some way beyond. Vampires '66' and '67' were sold in 1971 and 1972 respectively, whilst '71' was retained by the RAF following its service with the CAACU. The ill-fated aircraft was allocated to the CFS and later joined the 'Vintage Pair', presumably to replace XK624. As previously stated, it was destroyed in the collision at Mildenhall.
All Newark Air Museum

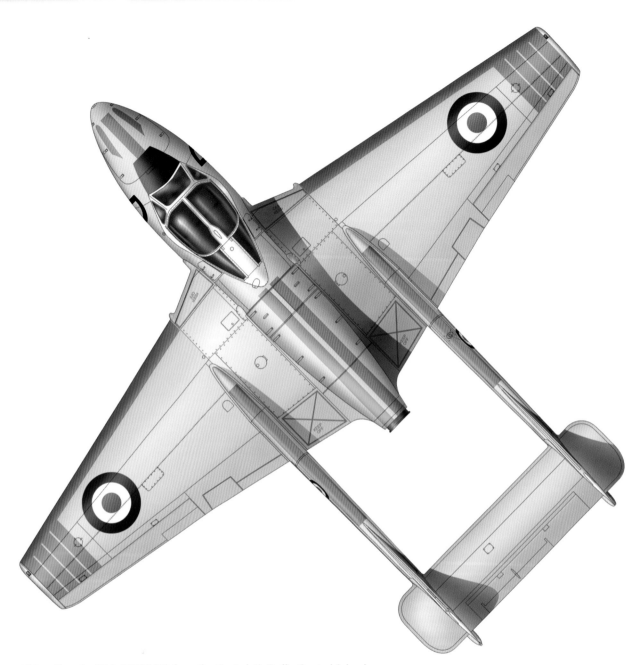

Vickers Vampire T.11, XE920 'D', from the Central Air Traffic Control School.
For further details please refer to page 70. Not to scale.

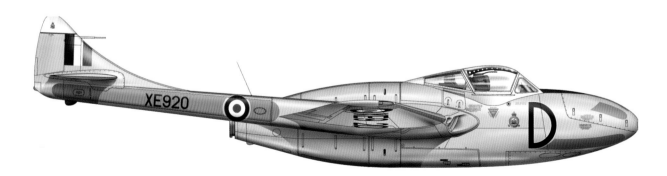

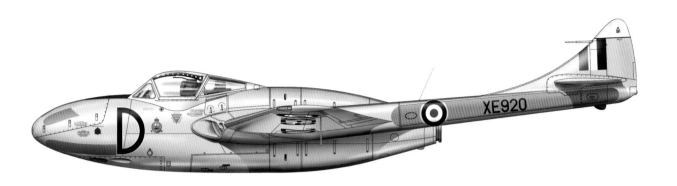

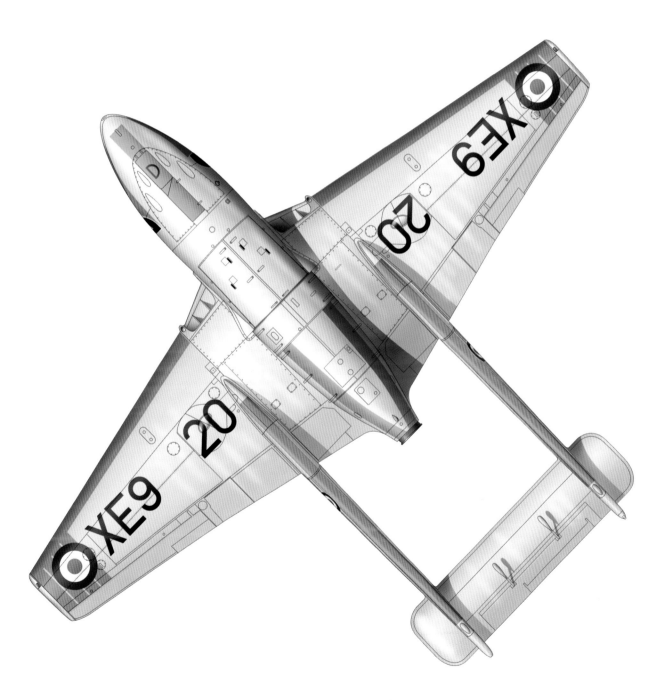

4   English Electric Canberra (Part 1)

The Canberra was designed by W E W Petter, and the eventual result of his and his team's labours was a twin-engined jet aircraft which, externally at least, comprised a reasonably straight-forward, perhaps even traditional design. Production orders were placed prior to the first flight of the prototype and, despite the inauspicious date of prototype VN799's first official flight; Friday 13 May 1949, the omens of ill-luck were to be disappointed and the Canberra went on to serve the RAF for 55 years, until 2006 in fact. Although the basic Canberra airframe would later be adapted for any number of differing yet essential duties, its initial operational roles were those as originally intended: bombing and photo-reconnaissance. There was a pressing need for a jet aircraft to replace existing piston-engined bombers, (and not simply the remaining Mosquito bombers), as well as a jet replacement for the remaining photo-reconnaissance Mosquito PR.34 and PR.34As, especially in Europe. The first RAF squadron to receive the Canberra was No.101 based at Binbrook which received B.2 WD936 on 25 May 1951, from which date the replacement of the Squadron's four-engined Avro Lincoln B.2s commenced. Number 540 Squadron at Benson received its first Canberra PR.3 in December 1952, thus becoming the first operational squadron to receive a dedicated photo-reconnaissance variant of this type.

As stated earlier in the introduction, the Canberra's development and operational history has been well catered for elsewhere, although seemingly fewer publications dealing with the Canberra in British service have been published throughout the last 50 years than with the Hunter. However, those Canberra books that were produced tend to be rather more comprehensive and, certainly in one instance, particularly authoritative and sought after. Given the existence of such titles it is not this author's intention to repeat the Canberra's history here. It is felt however, that some readers might benefit by the inclusion of a list categorising those marks of Canberra which entered production, including a list of subsequent marks introduced as a result of various modifications that justified the creation of new mark numbers. Additionally, a list of Canberra serial numbers is also provided.

The images in this section are arranged by aircraft serial in ascending order up to and including WJxxx; serial allocations from WKxxx and upwards will appear in volume two of this series.

Canberra Marks as built.
B.2, PR.3, T.4, B.6, B(I).6, PR.7, B(I).8, PR.9.

Canberra Conversions.
B.2T, B(TT).2, B.6 (BS), B.6(Mod), B.8, U.10 (later D.10), T.11, U.14 (later D.14), B.15, E.15, B.16, T.17, T.17A, TT.18, T.19, T.22,

Key to role letters: B = Bomber, B(I) = Bomber (Interdictor), BS = Blue Shadow (radar equipment), D = (unmanned) Drone, E = Electronic (radar and radio calibration), PR = Photo-Reconnaissance, T = Trainer, (and could as equally indicate a pilot trainer [T.4] as it could an ECM trainer [T.17 for instance.]) TT = Target Tug, U = Unmanned drone.

Canberra Serial Numbers. (Excludes
cancelled orders. Note, although all of the Canberras listed below were allocated British serial numbers, several amongst them were diverted almost immediately to fulfil foreign orders without having served the RAF and, in some instances, may never have worn their original serial numbers at all).

Prototype A.1s: VN799, VN813, VN828, VN850. Strictly these were English Electric A.1s but often referred to as Canberra B.1s.
Prototype B.2s: VX165, VX169.
Prototype PR.3: VX181.
Prototype B.5: VX185. Not proceeded with.
Prototype T.4: WN467.
Canberra B.2: WD929-WD966, WD980-WD999. WE111-WE122. WF886-WF892, WF907-WF917. WG788-WG789. WH637-WH674, WH695-WH742, WH853-WH887, WH902-WH925, WH944. WJ564-WJ582, WJ603-WJ649, WJ674-WJ682, WJ712-WJ734, WJ751-WJ753, WJ971-WJ995. WK102-WK146, WK161-WK165. WP514-WP515. WV787. XA536.
Canberra PR.3: WE135-WE151, WE166-WE175. WF922-WF928. WH772.
Canberra T.4: WE188-WE195. WH839-WH850. WJ857-WJ881. WT475-WT492. XH583-XH584.
Canberra B.6: WH945-WH984. WJ754-WJ784. WT205-WT213, WT301-WT306, WT369-WT374. XH567-XH570. XK641.
Canberra B(I).6: WT307-WT325, XG554. XJ249, XJ257.
Canberra PR.7: WH773-WH780, WH790-WH804. WJ815-WJ825. WT503-WT542.
Canberra B(I).8: WT326-WT348, WT362-WT368. XH203-XH209, XH228, XH231, XH234. XK951, XK952. XM244-XM245, XM262-XM279. XM936.
Canberra PR.9: XH129-XH137, XH164-XH177.

Opposite top and below:
Two images of prototype Canberra PR.3 VX181 at Finningley, September 1965. First flown in March 1951, this Canberra spent its entire active career as a test aircraft, principally with the A&AEE whose Motif is displayed on the fin. VX181 last flew in June 1969 when it was flown to RAF Pershore, Worcestershire, for use in a ground training role. It was subsequently scrapped. Apart from its resplendent colour scheme, the white lettering on the starboard side of the nose, although indistinct, may commemorate the two record flights set by this aircraft. In January 1953, VX181 flew from London to Darwin in 22 hours and 21 seconds, completing en-route a record time to Karachi of 8 hours 52minutes and 28 seconds.
Both author's collection

Top: *Canberra T.4 WD963. Originally built as a B.2 and first flown in early 1952, this aircraft served with a number of units until it was withdrawn for conversion to T.4 standard, one of 16 such conversions for the RAF supplementing their purpose-built T.4s. WD963 was subsequently transferred, on loan, to No.75 Squadron RNZAF, which began to receive Canberra B.2s from June 1958 at Coningsby, Lincolnshire, prior to deploying to Malaya a month later. This unit operated Canberras until March 1962, dating this photograph to a point somewhere between the two dates. Finished in overall High Speed Silver with yellow training bands, WD963 retained its standard RAF serial and national markings, embellished with a kiwi superimposed on a map of New Zealand applied to the fin. Having been returned to the RAF, this aircraft was last operated by No.45 Squadron until 29 June 1967, on which date it crashed near Tengah, Singapore, as a result of engine failure caused by fuel contamination.* Newark Air Museum

Above: *Canberra B.2 WE113, No.100 Squadron. Date and location not given. Delivered in June 1952, this Canberra served with No.231 OCU and then Nos.245, 98, 85 and 100 Squadron* prior to returning to No.231 OCU. It was placed in store at RAF Wyton in January 1992 and later scrapped, although the nose and cockpit section were preserved. The blue and white checks on WE113's fin contain No.100 Squadron's Motif, a skull and crossbones which appears on the Squadron Badge and whose motto translated reads 'Never stir up a hornet's nest'. WE113 was one of at least seven B.2s converted to become B(TT).2s for the target tug role.* Newark Air Museum

Opposite top: *Canberra WE146, RAE Llanbedr, June 1974. Originally built as a PR.3 in 1953, this aircraft never entered RAF service and was retained for trials purposes. In 1967 it was modified by Shorts to become the launch platform for a supersonic target drone: the SD.2 Stiletto, seen here on the port wing pylon. Following this modification, WE146 was redesignated as an SD.1 and stationed at Llanbedr, where it continued to serve until struck off charge in April 1975. The Stiletto went on to be operated by No.100 Squadron which reformed at West Raynham in 1972, as a target facilities unit equipped with Canberras.* Newark Air Museum

Below centre: *Canberra PR.3 WE166, No.231 OCU, seen at Waddington, 14 September, 1963. Delivered in October 1953, this aircraft was operated in turn by Nos.231, 237 and 231 OCUs. It was broken up in July 1970 and sold for scrap six months later. The leopard's head upon a white shield seen on WE166's fin is No.231 OCU's motif extracted from the Unit's Badge; their motto being 'Prepared to attack'. Number 231 OCU reformed on 1 December 1951 at Bassingbourn, Cambridgeshire, to train Canberra crews and absorbed Bassingbourn-based No.237 (Photographic Reconnaissance) OCU at the same time, (though sources conflict regarding the precise date of the absorption). Their first Canberras didn't arrive until February 1952, so Mosquitos and Meteors were retained for a time. Number 231 OCU moved to Cottesmore, Rutland in 1968, then Marham, Norfolk in 1976 and Wyton in 1982. In December 1990, whilst at Wyton, it was redesignated to become the Canberra Standardisation Training Flight; however, this was short-lived and it reverted to No.231 OCU six months later until finally disbanded on 23 April 1993. In the interim, No.237 (Photographic Reconnaissance) OCU reformed in October 1956, at Wyton, from No.231's 'C' (PR) Squadron, until, in January 1958, No.237 once again merged with No.231 OCU.* Newark Air Museum

Bottom: *Canberra PR.3 WE172, No.231 OCU, seen at the National Air Races, Baginton, Coventry, 18 August 1962. Delivered in October 1953 and operated in turn by Nos.231, 237 and 231 OCUs, it was sold to the British Aircraft Corporation (BAC) in 1965 and subsequently sold on to Venezuela.* Chris Salter collection

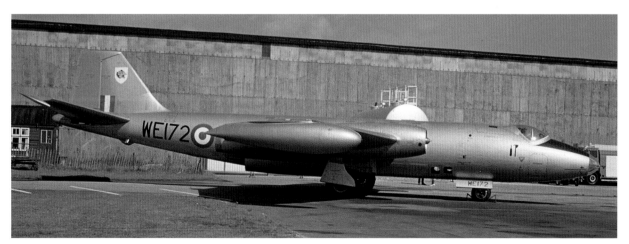

Top: *Canberra T.4 WE188, date and location not specified. WE188 was first flown in July 1952 and was also the first production T.4 built. This aircraft served with several units including station flights at Hemswell, Waddington, Upwood and Wyton; Nos.56, 100 and 360 Squadrons and No.231 OCU. It was sold in November 1981 to BAC who flew it several times until placing it in storage. It was sold into preservation in 1988.* Author's collection

Above: *Canberra B.2 WF907 / 7386M, No.1 School of Technical Training (SoTT), Halton, June or July 1966. WF907 was delivered in July 1952 and enjoyed an operational life of just over four years serving with Nos.9 and 100 Squadrons before being allocated to No.1 SoTT. Initially it was to have received the maintenance serial 7380M, but this was not taken up and received the serial 7386M instead, although in this image it is simply rendered as 7386. In 1968 7386M was removed to Halton's fire dump and had expired by 1971.* Author's collection

Below: *Canberra B.2 WH657, date and location not specified, but might possibly be Cranfield, Bedfordshire, circa 1967-69. Delivered in November 1952, this aircraft was first issued to No.231 OCU, although by mid-1953 it was with the National Gas Turbine Establishment for investigation into fuel feed development and high altitude engine problems. For four years from 1962, WH657 was used to track British satellites, following which it participated in slush trials at the College of Aeronautics, Cranfield, Bedfordshire. In April 1969 the B.2 was allocated to RFD Ltd (Reginald Foster Dagnall) at Godalming, Surrey, which produced lifejackets and other items of lifesaving equipment for airline and shipping companies. In 1977 RFD Ltd bought WH657, retaining it until it was sold into preservation in 1986.* Author's collection

Bottom: *Canberra T.17 WH664 'EH', No.360 Squadron, Wyton, 28 April 1990. Delivered in December 1952, this aircraft was first operated by No.231 OCU but in late 1959 was allocated to Swifter Flight (some sources state Squadron) which formed in January 1960 at El Adem, Libya. Its purpose was to investigate low-altitude, high-speed flight in hot climates and its effects on aircrew and airframes, for which the six Canberra B.2s involved required strengthening to deal with the stresses expected. The data so obtained was also expected to be used in the TSR.2 programme. Later, WH664 was converted to T.17 standard, one of 24 such conversions – six of which were later upgraded to become T.17As. The T.17 was fitted with a new and distinctive nose and optimised for ECM and EW (Electronic Warfare) training for the RAF and RN as well as (later) other NATO air forces. The T.17s were operated by a joint RAF/RN unit – No.360 Squadron, which formed on 1 April 1966 at Watton, Norfolk, although their first T.17 didn't arrive until the following December. The squadron moved to Cottesmore in April 1969, then to Wyton on 1 September 1975 and disbanded there on 31 Oct 1994; its role being assumed by the civil contractors, Flight Refuelling Ltd. In this image WH664 displays No.360 Squadron's red bar with lightning flash to each side of the fuselage roundel, plus the Squadron Motif on the fin consisting of a moth upon a trident; the motto 'Confundemus' translated reads 'We shall throw into confusion'. WH664 was scrapped at Wyton in July 1992.* Newark Air Museum

Top: *Canberra B(TT).2 WH666, No.56 Squadron. Delivered in December 1952 as a B.2, this aircraft was operated by Nos.10 and 45 Squadrons prior to being loaned to No.75 Squadron RNZAF from July 1958 until January 1962. Upon its return to the RAF, WH666 was operated by the CFE's Fighter Command Target Facilities Squadron at West Raynham, presumably in the TT role, it being certain that this B.2 became one of the seven or so that acquired the semi-official designation B(TT).2. On 1 April 1963, the Fighter Command Target Facilities Squadron was redesignated No.85 Squadron, intended to provide aircraft for fighter intercept training duties. Prior to that date, WH666 had joined No.56 Squadron whose colours and Motif are visible in this image on the nose and tail fin. This was a Lightning-equipped fighter squadron which moved to Cyprus in 1967 and, although few squadron histories mention it, they took their Canberras with them, including WH666, presumably to provide their own target facilities flight. Later, this aircraft served with No.100 Squadron prior to being sold to Zimbabwe in 1981.* Tony Buttler collection

Above: *Canberra B.2 WH673, RAFFC, seen at Syerston, Nottinghamshire, September 1957. Delivered in January 1953, this Canberra was first operated by the RAFFC at Manby, Lincolnshire and, other than a two year period seconded to Boulton Paul from January 1961 to May 1963, WH673's active life was completed at the RAFCAW Manby. (The RAFCAW was formed in July 1962 by renaming the RAFFC). From July 1966 it was placed in store until issued for ground instructional use at Farnborough in late 1973. Thereafter, either the whole airframe or sections of it went to the Air Weapons Research Establishment (AWRE) at Foulness in 1980. Its remains are believed to have been scrapped there in early 1994.* Newark Air Museum

Below: *Canberra B.2 WH703 'U', No.100 Squadron undergoing inspection circa 1973-75, possibly at West Raynham. Delivered in February 1953, this aircraft served in turn with No.231 OCU, No.85 and No.100 Squadron, No.231 OCU and finally with No.100 Squadron once more. In January 1976, No.100 Squadron moved to Marham, remaining there until it moved to Wyton in* *January 1982, where the Squadron finally relinquished Canberras for Hawk T.1As from late 1991. As for WH703, it became ground instructional airframe 8490M in March 1976, just two months after arriving at Marham. Subsequently it was transferred to the Battle Damage Repair Flight (BDRF) at Abingdon and was scrapped elsewhere by March 1994. All author's collection*

Top: *Canberra PR.7 WH796 'O', date, unit and location not specified. First flown in 1954, this aircraft was ordered as one of 24 PR Canberras built within serial batches WH772-WH780 and WH790-WH804; the first however, (WH772), was completed as a PR.3 whilst the remainder were PR.7s. WH796 served with a number of units including No.13 Squadron and, although it is difficult to positively identify, the motif seen on the fin seems likely to belong to that Squadron whose Badge and Motif featured a lynx's head superimposed upon a dagger; their motto translated reads 'We assist by watching'. WH796 went into storage in 1971 and it apparently remained stored until sold 10 years later.* Tony Buttler collection

Above: *Canberra T.4 WH842, 1966/67, unit and location not specified. Delivered in April 1954, WH842 was operated by No.231 OCU, No.88 Squadron, No.80 Squadron and the Bruggen Station Flight. It was struck off charge on 23 November 1971 and despatched to the Fire Fighting School at Catterick, North Yorkshire in 1972.* Chris Salter collection

Top: *Canberra T.11 WH904, No.85 Squadron, Binbrook,
September 1964. Delivered as a B.2 in February 1954, WH904
was operated by Nos.207 and No.35 Squadrons prior to being
converted to T.11 standard; one of eight such conversions,
(excluding WJ734 - the trials aircraft) all of which survived to be
later converted to T.19 standard. The T.11's primary role, initially
at least, was as an airborne radar trainer for the radar equipped
all-weather Gloster Javelin crews, although the T.11's duties
ultimately became more diverse and they later operated as targets
for Lightnings and Bloodhound SAM missiles too. It was the fitting
of the radar that gave this mark such a distinctive nose profile.*
Author's collection

Above: *Canberra T.11 (or T.19?) WH904 'D', No.85 Squadron,
Binbrook, (see WH666 for details No.85 Squadron's duties).
Although undated this is a later image than the previous judging by
the colour scheme and application of Day-Glo; it is also possible
that WH904 was by this time a T.19. The conversion from T.11 to
T.19 standard commenced in 1965, with the last completed in
1969 and entailed the removal of the radar and associated
equipment. A comparison of the two images shows the Squadron's
Badge applied aft of the cockpit in the first image with their
coloured checks on the fuselage. In the second, the Badge is deleted
but the Squadron's hexagonal Motif appears on the fin. Today
WH904 resides at Newark Air Museum.* Author's collection

Top: *Canberra B.6 (Mod) WH953, Boscombe Down, 10 June 1990. Delivered as a B.6 on 2 February 1955, WH953 was delivered to RRE Defford, Worcestershire, to commence a career in radar research programmes and was removed from RAF charge on the same day. In 1959 it was transferred to RRE Pershore where it was modified to receive an extended nose and, thereafter, returned to radar research programmes for much of the remainder of its active life which included involvement in the testing of the Panavia* Tornado F.2/F.3 radar system. When this photograph was taken in 1990, WH953 had a very distinctive, irregularly shaped area of red paint missing from the port side leading edge of the fin. Author's collection

Above: *Canberra B.6 (Mod) WH953, Boscombe Down, 10 June 1990. A less flattering view. WH953 appears to have continued flying until at least 1993.* Author's collection

Above: *Canberra B.6 WH973, No.9 Squadron, date and location not provided. Delivered in October 1955, this aircraft first served with No.9 Squadron, following which it was modified to become a B.15, one of 38 production conversions - eight of which were later modified to E.15 standard, including WH973. The E.15 was, in essence, a B.15 with improved electronic equipment, whilst the B.15 itself was an improved B.6 which incorporated an enhanced navigation and weapons fit. In this image, WH973 stands in front of a Royal Canadian Air Force, Canadair North Star transport, which displays the earlier Canadian National Flag on its fin rather than the current design, which at least dictates that this image pre-dates 15 February 1965! WH973 prominently displays the*

Squadron bat Motif on tail-fin and tip-tank with a lightning flash on its nose; this aircraft crashed on approach to Cottesmore on 6 October 1971, (some state 5 October), whilst on the strength of No.98 Squadron. All three crew members escaped safely. Tony Buttler collection

Below: *Canberra E.15 WH981 'CN', Wyton, 1993. A cheerless image of an aircraft originally delivered in 1955 as a B.6 and twice modified to B.15 and later E.15 standard, (see also WH973 re these marks). Its last unit was No.100 Squadron at Wyton where it was broken up in September 1993. Its component parts were scrapped in Essex in 1995.* Newark Air Museum

Below: *Canberra B.2 WJ573, RAF Technical College, Henlow, Bedfordshire, May 1963. Delivered in May 1953, this aircraft served first with No.540 Squadron, with which unit it has been suggested, it and two other B.2s were involved in high-level flights over the Soviet Union during August 1953! Next, WJ573 joined No.1323 Flight which reformed in October 1953 at Wyton having previously been titled as 2TAF Tactical Development Unit, equipped with four, later six, B.2s. The Flight continued in existence until 1 November 1955, when it became No.542 Squadron, retaining WJ573. Later, WJ573 joined Swifter Flight (see T.17, WH664), following which it went to Henlow in October 1960 and was allocated the maintenance serial 7656M in December that year. Although later assigned to the RAF Museum at Henlow, it was apparently scrapped some years later.* Newark Air Museum

Bottom: *Canberra B.2 WJ678 'G', No.85 Squadron, mid-1960s. Awaiting collection from the end of January 1955, WJ678 spent the early years of its life trialling various modifications and undergoing winterisation trials in Canada from November 1956. An extended period of storage commenced from November 1957 until issued to No.85 Squadron which reformed in 1963. WJ678 went on to serve with No.100 squadron until allocated to the BDRF at Abingdon in June 1985. Acquiring the serial 8864M during the following November, it was scrapped in 1994.*
Newark Air Museum

Top: *Canberra B.2 WJ678 'G', No.85 Squadron, Binbrook, mid-1960s, seen arriving at the runway's threshold. Beyond, Meteor F.8s are evident; they were also part of No.85 Squadron's complement and remained so until July 1970.*
Newark Air Museum

Above: *Canberra B.2 WJ728, No.100 Squadron, circa 1973. Delivered in January 1954, WJ728 served with a number of squadrons, but No.100 Squadron was the last with which it flew. It was transferred to the RAE for ground instructional duties and broken up in March 1984.* Tony Buttler collection

Opposite top: *Canberra B.2's WJ731 and WJ677, No.231 OCU, circa 1973. Contrary to alpha-numerical expectation, WJ731 was delivered in December 1953, whilst WJ677 was delivered in February 1955. Both served with several units prior to joining No.231 OCU as seen here. This image was taken before November 1975, the date that WJ677 left No.7 Squadron, its final employer, and arrived at Yeovilton to be struck off charge and put onto the firedump. WJ731 remained in service for many more years and was later posted to No.7 Squadron, prior to returning to No.231 OCU, (its final unit) coded 'BK'. Additionally, at some point – but certainly by September 1981, a disruptive Dark Green / Dark Sea Grey camouflage scheme had been applied which was retained to the end. Reportedly, WJ731 became the last operational B.2 in RAF*

service and made its final flight on 8 July 1993. It had been scrapped at Wyton by April 1994. The cockpit sections from both aircraft were preserved. Author's collection

Opposite bottom: *Canberra T.4 WJ870, seen over Finningley, September 1965. Delivered in November 1954, this Canberra offers no visible clues as to which unit was operating it when this photograph was taken; it does however emphasise a work-stained condition in stark contrast to the many pristine Canberra images that exist. On 16 April 1981 WJ870 was passed to the BDRF at St Mawgan, Cornwall, and had been scrapped by 1992.* Author's collection

Top: *Canberra T.4 WJ878 / 7636M '19', No.1 SoTT, Halton, July 1966. Delivered on 10 February 1955, WJ878 spent its first year or so involved in trials prior to joining No.231 OCU. In May 1960 it was flown to Halton and joined its fleet of ground instructional airframes. Serialed 7636M, as seen in this image, it was scrapped in 1974. To the rear of the Canberra appears the nose of a Hunting Percival Provost T.1 coded '28'. The Canberra code '19' and Provost code '28' have been applied in house, by No.1 SoTT.* Newark Air Museum

Above: *Canberra T.4 WJ879, No.58 Squadron, Wyton, 14 September 1963. Delivered two days prior to WJ878, WJ879 spent two periods of service with No.58 Squadron whose Motif, an owl, can be seen upon the fin as indeed it does on the PR Canberra beyond. Their motto translated reads 'On the wings of the night', and refers to the unit's night-bombing role during both world wars as well as the inter-war period. Disbanded in May 1945, the Squadron reformed as a PR unit on 1 October 1946 and later operated Canberra PR.3, PR.7 and PR.9 variants before disbanding again in September 1970. WJ879's final unit was No.231 OCU, coded 'BH' and, as with so many elderly Canberras, it was scrapped at Wyton in December 1992.* Newark Air Museum

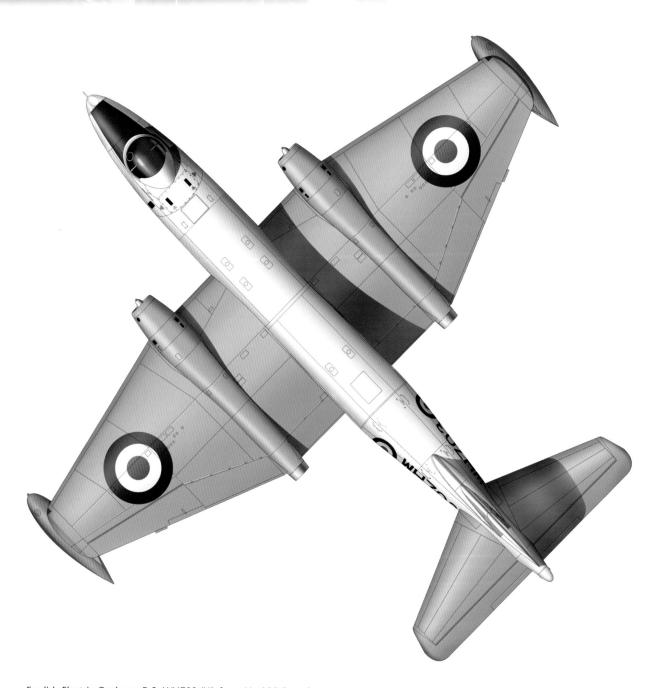

English Electric Canberra B.2, WH703 'U', from No.100 Squadron.
For further details please refer to page 83. Not to scale.

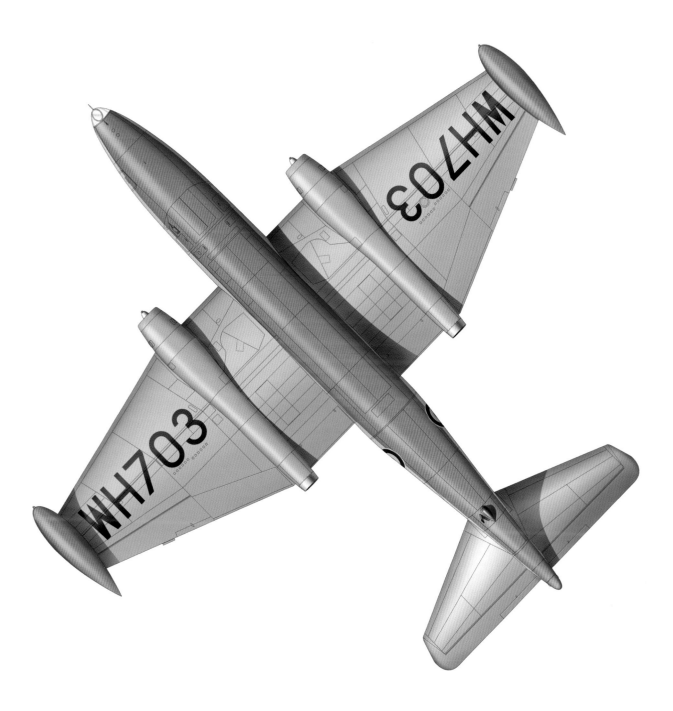

Top: *Canberra T.17 WJ986. Built and delivered as a B.2 on 16 October 1953, this aircraft became one of 24 T.17 conversions and was delivered to No.360 Squadron at Watton in March 1967. It is believed that this image dates from that period, certainly WJ986 appears to be in pristine condition. In comparison to WH664 (see page 81), this Canberra seems devoid of any unit markings or codes, although later all would be applied in full measure, as would, later still, the Hemp colour scheme. WJ986 was scrapped at Wyton in January 1995.* Author's collection

Above: *Three unidentified Canberras in flight. Waddington, 19 September 1964.* Newark Air Museum

AIRCRAFT & ENGINES
Armstrong-Siddeley Sapphire (engine): 29
Avro Lancaster: 13, 18
Avro Lincoln: 76
Avro York: 10
Blackburn Bucanneer: 37
Bristol Hercules (engine): 11, 20
British Aircraft Corporation TSR.2: 30, 81
Canadair North Star: 87
Canadair (built) Sabre: 24, 33, 34
Curtiss Kittyhawk: 35
Curtiss Tomahawk: 35
De Havilland Mosquito: 73, 76, 79
De Havilland Vampire: 33
   FB.5: 9, 64
   FB.9: 9
   NF.10: 64
   T.11: 8-9, 64-75
   T.22: 65
De Havilland Sea Vampire T.22: 65
Douglas Dakota: 11, 12, 13
English Electric Canberra (pt.1): 7, 76
   A.1 ('B.1' Prototypes): 77
   B.2: 76-78, 80-83, 88-89, 91,
   B.2(T): 77
   B(TT)2: 77-78, 82,
   PR.3: 76-79, 84, 91
   T.4: 77-78, 80, 84, 91
   B.5: 77
   B.6: 77, 86, 87
   B.6(Mod): 77, 86
   B.6(BS): 77
   B(I)6: 6, 77,
   PR.7: 77, 84, 91
   B.8: 77
   B(I)8: 8, 77,
   PR.9: 77, 91
   U.10/D.10: 77
   T.11: 77, 85
   U.14/D.14: 77
   B.15/E.15: 77, 87
   B.16: 77
   T.17/T.17A: 77, 81, 94
   TT.18: 77
   T.22: 77
English Electric Lightning: 28, 46, 49, 82, 85
Folland Gnat: 69
Gloster Meteor: 67, 79
   F.8: 24, 89
   T.7: 46, 72
   U.16/D.16: 30
Gloster Javelin: 24, 72, 85
Handley Page Hastings: 13
Handley Page Marathon: 67
Hawker Hunter: 7, 24-63
   Prototypes: 24
   F.1: 25-26, 28-29
   F.2: 25, 29
   Mk.3: 28-29
   F.4: 25, 29-30, 34-35, 41-42, 56, 58-59
   F.5: 25-26, 29
   F.6: 7, 25-26, 28-30, 32-24, 37-41, 43-45, 48-49
   F.6A: 30, 33, 44
   T.7: 28-29, 35, 46-47, 49, 52, 55, 60
   T.7A: 30, 46
   T.8: 30, 56, 58, 60
   T.8B: 28, 30, 60
   T.8C: 28, 30, 42, 56, 61
   T.8M:
   FGA.9: 8, 25, 28, 30, 32, 37-38, 41-41, 48, 50-53, 55, 56
   FR.10: 25, 30, 39, 44-45, 50, 53, 55
   GA.11: 30, 59
   PR.11: 30, 59
   Mk.12: 30, 32
   Mk.58: 28, 30, 61
Hawker P.1052: 24
Hawker P.1067: 29
Hawker P.1081: 24
Hawker P.1083: 29
Hawker-Siddeley Andover: 53
Hawker-Siddeley Hawk: 83
Hawker-Siddeley Sea Harrier: 30, 61

Hunting-Percival Jet Provost: 69, 70
Hunting-Percival Provost: 34, 67, 91
McDonnel-Douglas Phantom: 8
Lockheed F.16: 61
Mikoyan-Gurevich MiG-15: 24
North-Amercian F-86E Sabre: 24, 33-34
Rolls-Royce Avon (engine): 26, 29
Rolls-Royce nene (engine): 11
Vickers Warwick: 10, 11
Vickers Wellington: 10, 11
Vickers Valetta: 8, 10-23
   C.1: 10, 12-13, 17-20
   C.2: 14, 19, 20
   T.3: 13, 16-20
   T.4 15, 19-20
   C(VVIP).2: 11
Vickers Varsity: 11, 67, 70
Vickers Viking: 10, 11, 15
North Amercian F-86 Sabre: 24, 33, 34
Panavia Tornado: 86
Short SD.1: 78
Short SD.2 Stiletto (target drone): 78
Supermarine Attacker: 24

LOCATIONS
Abingdon: 17, 83, 88
Aden Protectorate: 50-55
Aeroventure (Doncaster): 19
Ahlhorn (W.Germany): 38
Aldbury (Herts): 18
Aqaba (Jordan): 18
Baginton (Warks): 79
Bassingbourn (Cambs): 79
Benina (Libya): 41
Benson (Oxon): 17,37
Bertam (Malaya): 18
Bicester (Oxon): 16
Binbrook (Lincs): 40, 85, 89
Boscombe Down (Wilts): 42, 86
Bracknell (Berks): 44
Brawdy (Pembs): 33, 44, 56, 68
Bruggen (W.Germany): 55
Cameron Highlands (Malaya): 18
Canada: 28, 88
Catterick (Yorks): 84
Changi (Singapore): 13, 18
Chile: 40, 52, 66, 69
Chippenham (Wilts): 18
Chivenor (Devon): 33
Church Fenton (Yorks): 65, 69
Clark Field (Philippines): 13
Colerne (Wilts): 13, 19
Coltishall (Norfolk): 37, 46
Coningsby (Lincs): 78
Cornwall: 43
Cosford (Salop): 19, 46
Cottesmore (Rutland): 79, 81, 87
Cranfield (Beds): 81
Cranwell (Lincs): 16, 19, 25, 37, 46, 69, 72
Cranwell North (Lincs): 25
Cyprus: 82
Defford (Worcs): 86
Deversoir (Egypt): 17
Devon: 53
Driffield (Yorks): 67, 69
El Adem (Libya): 81
Exeter (Devon): 35, 73
Fayid (Egypt): 17
Finningley (S.Yorks): 32, 39, 45, 77, 91
Foulness (Essex): 82
Gatow (Berlin): 14
Gemas, Mt Ophir (Malaya): 18
German Democratic Republic: 24
Gibraltar: 8
Gutersloh (W.Germany): 38
Halton (Bucks): 7, 34-35, 80
Hartland Point (N.Devon): 18
Hatfield (Herts): 67, 72
Hendon (Gtr London): 11, 39
Henlow (Beds): 26, 88
Hereford: 18
Hucknall (Notts): 69
Imperial War Museum (London): 66

Ipoh (Malaya): 18
Iraq: 29
Isle of Wight: 56
Jebel al Lawz (Saudi Arabia): 18
Jordan: 38, 39
Karachi (Pakistan): 77
Kelvedon Hatch (Essex): 30
Kemble (Glos): 67
Keogh Barracks (Hants): 44
Khormaksar (Aden): 30, 35, 50-56
Kuala Lumpur (Malaya): 17
Kuwait: 38
Lebanon: 28, 30
Leconfield (Yorks): 7, 69, 72
Leeming (Yorks): 65
Leuchars (Fife): 26
Linton-on-Ouse (Yorks): 24, 65
Little Rissington (Glos): 72
Llandow (Glamorgan): 73
Loka (Sudan): 17
Lossiemiuth (Moray): 44, 51, 58-59
Luqa (Malta): 18
Lyme Regis (Dorset): 28
Lyneham (Wilts): 17-18
Malaya: 13, 17, 78
Manby (Lincs): 82
Melton Mowbray (Leics): 42
Melun-Villaroche (France): 70
Mildenhall (Suffolk): 72
Mombasa (Kenya): 51
Montrose (Angus): 69
Moreton-in-Marsh (Glos): 59
New Zealand: 78
Newark Air Museum (Notts): 8, 85
Nicosia (Cyprus): 10
Norfolk & Suffolk Aviation Museum: 19
North Luffenham (Rutland): 12
Odiham (Hants): 12, 17
Oman: 39
Otterburn Ranges (Nthmlnd): 37
Perak (Malaya): 18
Pershore (Worcs): 77
Saudi Arabia: 29
Scampton (Lincs): 28
Shawbury (Shrops): 65, 70, 72
Singapore: 41, 45
Singapore Island: 18
South Africa: 33
St Mawgan (Cornwall): 91
Stockholm (Sweden): 17
Swinderby (Lincs): 64, 67, 70
Syerston (Notts): 42, 65, 82
Tengah (Singapore): 78
Upper Heyford (Oxon): 37
Valley (Anglesey): 7, 64
Venezuela: 79, 95
Waddington (Lincs): 16, 30, 79
Waterbeach (Cambs): 37
Watton (Norfolk): 81, 94
West Raynham (Norfolk): 30, 37, 40, 43, 78, 82, 83
Wildenrath (W.Germany): 24
Winthorpe (Notts): 8
Wisley (Surrey): 11
Wyton (Hunts): 13, 20, 47, 78-79, 81, 83, 87-88, 91, 94
Yatesbury (Wilts): 26
Yeovilton (Somerset): 35, 56, 58-59, 66, 91
Zimbabwe: 82

BRITISH FLYING & TRAINING UNITS
plus Support and Research Establishments
A&AEE (Boscombe Down): 14-15, 19, 26, 34, 39, 77
Aden Strike Wing: 50
Advanced Flying Schools:
   202 AFS: 64
   203 AFS: 67
Aero Flight (RAE Bedford): 30
Air Direction Training Unit: 58, 66
Air Electronics School: 15
Air Navigation Schools:
   1 ANS: 15, 17-18
   2 ANS: 15-16, 18, 20
   3 ANS: 15

5 ANS: 15, 17
6 ANS: 15, 17
Air Weapons Research Establishment (AWRE): 82
Airwork Limited: 66-67
Allied Air Forces Central Europe Comms Flt: 70
Central Air Traffic Control School (CATCS): 13, 65, 69, 70
Central Fighter Establishment (CFE): 26, 29-30, 37, 40, 69, 82
Central Flying School (CFS): 65, 69, 72
Central Gunnery School (CGS): 69
Central Navigation & Control School (CNCS): 13
Central Servicing Development Establishment (CSDE): 16
Civil Anti-Aircraft Co-operation Units:
　3 CAACU: 73
　4 CAACU: 73
　3/4 CAACU: 35, 65, 73
Day Fighter Leaders School (DFLS): 26, 37, 43, 45
Display Teams:
　Black Arrows (111 Sqn): 48
　Blue Diamonds (92 Sqn): 49
　Vintage Pair (CFS): 65, 72-73
Empire Test Pilots School: 17, 28, 37, 41, 55
Far East Transport Wing: 18
Fighter Combat School: 30, 37, 40
Fighter Weapons School: 69
Fire Fighting School: 84
Fleet Air Arm: 42, 55, 57-61, 65
Fleet Air Arm Squadrons:
　736: 67
　738: 59, 67
　759: 42
　764: 59
　899: 61
Fleet Requirements & Air Direction Unit (FRADU): 42, 56, 59
Flying Training Schools:
　1 FTS: 65, 69
　3 FTS: 65, 69
　4 FTS: 7, 37, 43, 45, 47, 69
　5 FTS: 65, 67, 69-70
　7 FTS: 65, 69
　8 FTS: 64, 67, 69, 70
Maintenance Units:
　27 MU (Shawbury): 69
　71 MU (Bicester): 16
Metropolitan Sector Operations Centre: 30
Ministry of Aviation: 16
Ministry of Defence / MoD(PE): 28, 47
Ministry of Supply: 11, 13, 26, 35, 37, 56
Operational Conversion Units:
　228 OCU: 15, 20, 67
　229 OCU: 7, 8, 26, 30, 32-33, 37, 39-44, 47, 52, 59, 65
　231 OCU: 78-81, 83-84, 91
　237 OCU: 33, 46, 79
　238 OCU: 15
　240 OCU: 12
　242 OCU: 17
Radio School, No.2: 26
RAE Bedford: 30
RAE Farnborough: 30, 32, 35, 37, 82
RAE Llanbedr: 30, 78
RAF College (RAFC): 9, 15-17, 19-20, 37, 69
RAF College of Air Warfare (RAFCAW): 12, 82
RAF Commands:
　Air Support Command: 12, 19
　Fighter Command: 24, 30
　Transport Command: 12, 19, 41
　38 Group: 41, 56
RAF Flights:
　2(TAF) HQ Flt: 35
　1312 Flt: 13
　1323 Flt: 88
　1417 Flt: 30, 35, 50, 52-53
　Aden CF (Comms Flt): 15
　Air HQ Malta Comms Flt: 18
　Battle Damage Repair Flt: 83, 88, 91
　Brawdy SF (Station Flt): 66
　Bruggen SF: 84
　Canberra Standardisation Trng Flt: 67
　Flag Officer Flying Trng Flt: 79

Hemswell SF: 80
Heron Flight: 35
King's Flight: 11
Laarbruch SF: 37, 55
Linton-on-Ouse SF: 65
Odiham SF: 65
Queen's Flight: 11
Swifter Flight: 81, 88
Upwood SF: 80
Waddington SF: 80
Weapon Instructor Flight: 40
West Raynham SF: 43
Wyton SF: 80
RAF Flying College (RAFFC): 15, 17, 82
RAF Squadrons:
　1: 25, 28-30, 33, 41-43, 54, 56
　2: 30, 45
　3: 29
　4: 28-30, 45
　7: 91
　8: 30, 50, 52, 55
　8/43: 35, 52, 55
　9: 80, 87
　10: 82
　13: 84
　14: 7, 29, 38, 59
　16: 64
　19: 29, 44
　20: 29-30, 37
　24: 14, 15
　26: 9, 29, 38, 41
　28: 30
　30: 13, 15, 17-18
　34: 25, 29
　35: 85
　41: 29
　43: 8, 26, 29-30, 33-34, 38, 50, 53
　45: 30, 42, 48, 55, 78, 82
　48: 13, 18
　52: 13, 17
　54: 8, 28-30, 33, 39-42, 56, 59
　56: 26, 29, 35, 37, 42, 64, 80, 82-83
　58: 30, 48, 91
　63: 29, 37, 40, 42-43, 45
　65: 29, 33, 37, 45, 49
　66: 24, 29, 37, 42, 45
　67: 24, 29
　70: 13, 15, 18
　71: 29, 35
　72: 72
　74: 29, 33, 43, 46
　78: 13, 17
　80: 84
　84: 13, 15-16, 18
　85: 78, 82, 83, 85, 88-89
　88: 84
　92: 24, 29, 34, 37, 49
　93: 29, 45
　98: 29, 78, 87
　100: 78, 80, 82-82, 87, 88
　101: 76
　110: 13, 18
　111: 29, 33, 43, 48-49
　112: 29, 35
　114: 10, 15
　115: 13, 15
　118: 9, 29
　122: 40
　130: 29, 34-35, 41
　167: 13
　173: 13
　187: 13
　204: 13
　205: 13
　207: 85
　208: 25, 29-30, 38-39, 42, 46, 50, 52, 55, 56
　216: 13, 18
　222: 26, 29
　233: 13, 15
　234: 29, 33, 41, 44, 47
　245: 29, 78
　247: 29, 40
　253: 64

　257: 29
　263: 29, 44
　360: 80-81, 94
　540: 76, 88
　542: 88
　617: 13
　622 (RAuxAF): 13
　683: 13
　Air Fighting Development Sqn: 29, 40, 42
　Day Fighter Combat Sqn: 30, 37, 40, 43, 45
　Ferry Support Sqn: 15
　Fighter Command Instrument Rating Sqn: 47
　Fighter Command Target Facilities Sqn: 82
RAF Staff College: 44
RAF Technical College: 88
Royal Auxiliary Air Force: 65
Royal Radar Establishment (RRE): 16, 28, 30, 77, 86
School of Technical Training, No.1 (SoTT): 34-35, 41, 80-81
Tactical Weapons Unit (TWU): 33, 43-44, 47-48, 52
　1TWU: 44, 47, 51-52
　2TWU: 44, 47, 51-52, 55
Telecommunications Research Establishment (TRE): 14

OVERSEAS FLYING UNITS
Indian Air Force: 29-30, 55
Jordanian Air Force: 38-39
Lebanese Air Force: 30
Royal Canadian Air Force (RCAF): 87
Royal New Zealand Air Force (RNZAF): 67
　75 Sqn: 78, 82
Royal Norwegian Air Force: 67
Royal Saudi Air Force: 33
Royal Swedish Air Force: 15
Royal Rhodesian Air Force: 67
Southern Rhodesian Air Force: 67
Swiss Air Force: 28, 34-35
Zimbabwe: 82

PERSONNEL & MISCELLANEOUS ITEMS
30mm ADEN Cannon: 25
Airwork Limited: 66-67
Bloodhound Surface-to-Air Missile: 85
Blue Fox radar: 30, 61
Boulton Paul Limited: 82
British Aircraft Corporation (BAC): 79-80
Churchill, Sir Winston: 10
College of Aeronautics: 81
Daily Mail Air Race: 46
Duke, Sqn Ldr Neville: 29
Fleet Air Arm Museum: 61
Flight Refuelling Limited: 81
Hawker Hunter Aviation Limited: 28, 42, 61
Hawker Siddeley Aviation: 30, 41
HMS Exeter: 56
London to Darwin Record Flight: 77
London to Paris Air Race: 46
National Gas Turbine Establishment: 81
North-East Aircraft Museum: 14
Northern Lights Combat Air Support: 28
Petter, W E W: 76
RAF Museum (Hendon): 11, 39
RAF Museum (Cosford): 19, 46
RFD Limited: 81
Riverside MoT Centre, Melksham (Wilts): 47
Rolls-Royce: 38
Smith, Mike: Curator Newark Air Museum: 8
Summers, J 'Mutt': 11
TACtical Air Naviation (TACAN): 30
'The Dam Busters': 11
Type B & D national markings: 59
Wade, Sqn Ldr T S: 24
Winterization Trials: 88